the british citizenship test
bernice walmsley

For over 60 years, more than
50 million people have learnt over
750 subjects the **teach yourself**
way, with impressive results.

be where you want to be
with **teach yourself**

For UK order enquiries: please contact Bookpoint Ltd, 130 Milton Park, Abingdon, Oxon, OX14 4SB. Telephone: +44 (0) 1235 827720. Fax: +44 (0) 1235 400454. Lines are open 09.00–17.00, Monday to Saturday, with a 24-hour message answering service. Details about our titles and how to order are available at www.teachyourself.co.uk

Long renowned as the authoritative source for self-guided learning – with more than 50 million copies sold worldwide – the **teach yourself** series includes over 500 titles in the fields of languages, crafts, hobbies, business, computing and education.

British Library Cataloguing in Publication Data: a catalogue record for this title is available from the British Library.

First published in UK 2007 by Hodder Education, 338 Euston Road, London, NW1 3BH.

This edition published 2007.

The **teach yourself** name is a registered trade mark of Hodder Headline.

Copyright © 2007 Bernice Walmsley

Official Home Office material reproduced in Chapters 3, 4, 5, 6 and 7 of this book is published with kind permission. Copyright © Crown 2007. This material has been reproduced under the terms of the Click-Use Licence.

Hodder Headline's policy is to use papers that are natural, renewable and recyclable products and made from wood grown in sustainable forests. The logging and manufacturing processes are expected to conform to the environmental regulations of the country of origin.

Impression number   10 9 8 7 6 5 4 3 2 1
Year   2010 2009 2008 2007

Thank you to the Teach Yourself team at Hodder – especially Lisa Grey – for their friendly help and guidance. I must also thank my husband William for his continuing support and patience, plus his invaluable attention to detail.

acknowledgements

v

contents

01

how this book will help you to pass the test

In this chapter you will:
- find out who needs to sit the British Citizenship Test
- examine how you can use this book
- learn a little about the British Citizenship Test.

Introduction

Why do we have a British Citizenship Test? Britain has a history of encouraging people from other countries to come here to settle and work. In order for immigrants to be able to do this successfully, the British Government believes that people applying for citizenship or for indefinite leave to remain need to be able to speak English and to possess some knowledge of the structures of British society, its culture and history. For this reason, the government introduced the British Citizenship Test in 2005. Since then over a quarter of a million people have taken the test.

> **Note**
>
> The British Citizenship Test is also known as the *Life in the UK Test* and is sometimes referred to simply as the *Citizenship Test*.

The British Citizenship Test is a straightforward test that you will need to pass in order to apply for naturalisation as a British citizen or for indefinite leave to remain.

> **Note**
>
> Indefinite leave to remain is also known as *settlement* or *permanent residence*.

There are no tricks or secrets in the test – it is an uncomplicated set of questions on material that has been produced by the Home Office and which is reproduced (with kind permission) in this book. So, if you have studied this book well there is no need to worry about taking the test. Understanding and learning the necessary information to answer the questions that you will be asked in the test is the most important thing to achieve, but you can also improve your chances of passing by becoming familiar with a few details about the test itself. This book will give you all the information you require: material you need to learn for the test, practice questions that will help you to prepare for the test and essential advice and tips on taking the test.

> **Note**
>
> The British Citizenship Test is usually taken in English, although special arrangements can be made for anyone who wants to take it in Welsh or Scottish Gaelic.

Who should read this book?

This book is intended to assist all those people who are considering applying for naturalisation (this is just another way of saying gaining citizenship of a country) as a British citizen or for indefinite leave to remain (this is, making your permission to stay permanent rather than applying to simply extend your existing visa). If English is your mother tongue and you have been living in the UK for several years, you might wonder whether you really have to read this book. The answer is yes – you will find the practice questions and advice about your application for citizenship or settlement very helpful.

Since 2005 you have had to take – and pass – the British Citizenship Test or attend classes before you can apply for naturalisation. From 2 April 2007, new rules have been introduced so that from this date people who are applying for indefinite leave to remain will also have to sit – and pass – this test. Although the test that people who are applying for citizenship and those who are applying for indefinite leave to remain is now the same, there is a difference between the two groups. If you are applying for citizenship, you will become a citizen of the UK. If you are applying for indefinite leave to remain (also known as settlement or permanent residence), you will not become a British citizen but will simply be allowed to stay in the country. If, at a later date, you decide to apply for citizenship you will not need to take the test again.

The British Citizenship Test is designed to test your knowledge of the structures and culture of British society and is considered essential by the government to an immigrant's successful integration into society. There is also a requirement – both for those seeking naturalisation and those seeking indefinite leave to remain – to demonstrate a satisfactory level of English. Again, this is believed to be necessary to live successfully in the UK.

If your standard of English is sufficient – i.e. ESOL Level 3 or above – you can take the British Citizenship Test. In dealing successfully with the required material and then passing this test you will have demonstrated an acceptable level of English, so you will not need to take any other test of your language abilities. If your standard of English is not up to this level then instead of taking the British Citizenship Test you will need to attend combined English language and citizenship classes, where you will not only study the materials about life in the UK but will also be developing your English language skills.

> **Note**
>
> Your local college of further education or a learndirect centre can give you an initial assessment of the standard of your English.

As a quick guide to the level of English required, generally you should be capable of holding a conversation in English on an unexpected topic. It should be workable English but it is not necessary to speak it perfectly. There will be more details about the language requirement in the next chapter (see page 14).

> **Note**
>
> If you are applying for citizenship, make sure you qualify to take the test before you go any further. It is necessary to have lived in the UK for five years for work-permit holders and three years for their dependants. Failure to fulfil this qualification is the main cause of failing the British Citizenship Test.

Apart from helping you to pass the British Citizenship Test, this book has a further aim in relation to people who wish to become British citizens or to gain settlement. There are many procedures and forms to navigate when you are applying and this book will help you. This book will also be useful for teachers, mentors, friends and family of people who are intending to apply for naturalisation or indefinite leave to remain and who are helping them in their efforts to achieve their aim.

Outline of the book's contents

This introductory chapter includes a few details about who this book is aimed at and how it can help them, as we have seen. In Chapter 2 we will look at what you need to do to prepare for your test and will answer questions you may have, such as 'Where do I find my nearest test centre?' and 'How can I be sure I have fulfilled all the legal requirements before taking the test?'

In Chapters 3, 4, 5, 6 and 7, five sections from the Home Office's book *Life in the United Kingdom – A Journey to Citizenship* will be reproduced (with kind permission). This material covers five main areas:

- A changing society – a summary of the history of immigration in the UK, the role of women and factors affecting young people.
- UK today: a profile – giving details of its population, religions, customs, traditions and regional differences.
- How Britain is governed – looking at how our constitution and institutions work and our place in Europe and the world.
- Everyday needs – dealing with everyday issues such as housing, education, health and leisure.
- Employment – all you need to know about finding work and applying for jobs, your rights at work, as well as childcare and the rights of children who work.

> **Note**
>
> It is vital that you study the correct edition of the official material. *Teach Yourself The British Citizenship Test* contains the very latest material – i.e. from the second edition of the official material (*Life in the United Kingdom – A Journey to Citizenship*). If you take your test on or after 2 July 2007, it will be based on this material. The first edition contained information that was different from the second edition, so it will not be helpful for you to study the first edition.

As well as this official material that you must learn, these chapters will also contain plenty of additional advice and help on using the material to best effect, as well as extra explanation where it is thought necessary. These additions to the Home Office material will always be outlined in a box to show that they are not part of the Home Office material. These are there to increase your understanding of the chapters and to improve your chances of passing the British Citizenship Test. They will also help to break up the material and give you some interesting pieces of information that will enhance your appreciation of the culture, history and background of the country in which you have chosen to live.

After you have studied this material you will come to a very important part of the book – the practice questions (Chapter 8). These will ensure that you know whether or not you have really understood and retained the material that you must learn. They are followed by three timed tests to enable you to check that not only have you learned the material, but also that you are able to answer the questions correctly in the allotted amount of time.

Having got through the practice questions and tests we will go on to discuss what happens after you have passed your Life in the UK Test. This will vary, of course, depending on whether you are aiming for naturalisation or settlement. If you are applying for citizenship you will need to take note of the information about the citizenship ceremony and about how to use your test pass to apply for citizenship. Once you've obtained British citizenship, you can then apply for a British passport. However, perhaps more importantly, depending on your current situation, Chapter 9 will explore what being a British citizen means – What are your rights and your responsibilities? How can you use your citizenship? Perhaps by voting in elections or becoming involved in your community if that is appropriate to your situation here. Whether you are aiming for indefinite leave to remain or for British citizenship, there are plenty of details and practical advice in Chapter 9 to help you with the processes you will have to go through to reach your final goal.

Finally, there is a section devoted to giving you plenty of sources of further information. Here you will find websites where you can find your nearest centre to sit the test, and where you will be able to download the relevant forms and check the latest procedures. If you do not have access to a computer and the internet, you will also find telephone numbers that you can call to get the further information you need. Note that many of these telephone helplines are completely free for you to use and there are even some helplines that will give you advice in a variety of languages so that as many people as possible can be helped.

> **Note**
> Public libraries are a useful source of information and you will also be able to gain access to the internet there.

Your path to British citizenship

> **Note**
> Some steps apply to both groups of people and others apply to either the group of people aiming at naturalisation and or to those applying for settlement.

figure 1 path to citizenship

How to use this book

There is a lot of information in this book: the material about life in the UK (Chapters 3, 4, 5, 6 and 7) that you will have to master specifically for the test, then the practice questions and answers, plus plenty of tips and advice to help you deal with it all. The aim is to make sure that your application is successful.

An organised approach is always best. If you work your way through each of the five chapters about life in the UK (Chapters 3, 4, 5, 6 and 7), testing yourself as you go, and then use the chapter about furthering your citizenship to appreciate what being a British citizen means, you will have given yourself the best opportunity for a positive result and a positive experience. If you are applying for indefinite leave to remain, this book will help you to pass this important test too – and you may also find it useful if you later go on to apply for naturalisation.

How to tackle learning for the test

Having learned that all the information you need to prepare for your test is in this book, you need to use the book well and to approach your learning in an organised and methodical way. To do this you should:

• Concentrate on one section at a time.
• Make sure you have fully understood each section before you move on to the next.
• Make notes on what you think are the most important parts of each section.
• Jot down dates and figures that you think may be the subject of the test questions.
• Test yourself as you go along.
• If there is anything you don't completely understand, try reading through the section again, summarising for yourself exactly what the sentence or paragraph is telling you.
• Try putting difficult sections into your own words. The effort of rephrasing even a very short sentence will often bring better understanding.
• If one section seems particularly difficult, use the practice questions relating to that section to help you (all the questions show clearly to which section of the Home Office materials they refer). Go back to the difficult section and find the

answer to each of the questions. The answers are all there and finding them will help you to understand the material better.

- Complete the timed tests so that you will be confident not only that you know the material, but also that you are able to complete the test in the time allowed.
- Try to find a mentor – this could be a teacher at a local college or a friend or relative with perhaps a better standard of English or more experience of life in the UK than you have.

Top tip

The very best advice you can be given if you want to pass the British Citizenship Test is – don't give up. There is no limit to the number of times you can sit the test.

Summary

In this introductory chapter we have looked at who will find this book useful and how you should use it to help in your preparations for the British Citizenship Test. The importance of the material supplied by the Home Office has been explained and you have been pointed in the right direction for success in the test. Now, all you need to do is to study and understand the material, then test yourself using the many practice questions that are supplied, then act on the advice given in Chapter 9. Good luck!

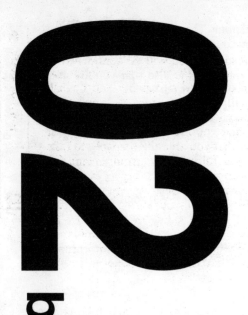

02

before your test

In this chapter you will:
- learn exactly how you can apply to take the test
- find out more about the standard of English required
- learn about the format of the test.

Introduction

The British Citizenship Test is the key to becoming a British citizen or achieving settlement. Until you have taken, and passed, this test (or taken a combined citizenship and English language course), you will not be able to apply for naturalisation, or for indefinite leave to remain, or for a British passport. So, it is essential that you are successful in this first step. This chapter will ensure that you are fully prepared to take the test – being sure that you fulfil all the requirements for citizenship or settlement and knowing what to expect at the test centre will give you the confidence you need to get through the test and will help to make it a less daunting experience. Preparation is all-important, so take a few moments to read about how you can prepare for the test – and how to apply for the test – before you get down to the serious business of learning the official Home Office material that is reproduced in the following chapters.

Who can apply to take the test?

The requirements for applying for British citizenship and those for applying for indefinite leave to remain are obviously different – but the test is the same. It is essential that you make sure you fulfil these requirements before applying to take the test. Bearing this in mind, let's look at these two groups of people separately:

Citizenship

There are some important conditions that you need to fulfil in your quest to become a British citizen. Unless you fulfil these requirements your application to become a British citizen will be rejected, so it is definitely worthwhile checking these conditions carefully before you start studying for your test.

- You must be 18 or over – the British naturalisation process is not designed to cover minors, as there are separate procedures for them.
- You must have lived in the UK for the qualifying residential period – the qualifying period is at least five years (or three years if you are married to a British citizen, providing you have a spouse visa, otherwise it is three years from the date you get married). This qualifying period is counted back from

the date of your application for citizenship, so on that date five years ago (or three years ago if appropriate) you must have been actually in the UK. You will normally prove your date by referring to the date stamp on your passport when you entered the UK. So, if your date stamp is less than five years before the date of your application (or three years if you are married to a British citizen) then you must delay your application. Many applications are automatically turned down each year because people have miscalculated or ignored the residency qualifying period.

- If you have, for any reason, spent a lot of time outside the UK during your qualifying residency period, this will be viewed unfavourably. There are set limits as to how much time you are allowed to spend outside the UK if you are applying for citizenship. You must not have been out of the UK for more than 90 days in the previous 12 months or for 450 days in the five years before the date of your application for citizenship. The rules are slightly different if you are applying as the spouse of a British citizen. If this is the case then the maximum amount of time that you are allowed to spend outside the UK prior to your date of application is 270 days in the previous three years.

- You must intend to settle in the UK – if you intend to go abroad for anything other than a holiday period (a week or two, maybe) then this may affect your citizenship application. The government requires that all new British citizens intend to continue being an active citizen, so leaving the country for anything other than a brief holiday or to work temporarily overseas for a company with British connections is not acceptable. Of course, it is not easy for anyone to assess your future intentions with any accuracy or certainty, but this is one of the stated requirements of citizenship.

- You must be of good character. Various checks will be carried out by the Home Office regarding your character and background. These could include police checks about any criminal convictions you have – your application may well be refused if you have lots of convictions, although the Home Office can use its discretion when assessing character and will take into account how long it is since the last offence was committed and the seriousness of the offences. Also included in the checks will be enquiries into your financial affairs – you are unlikely to be successful in your application if you are an undischarged bankrupt, for example – and your Income Tax records will also come under scrutiny.

- You must have good language skills – these are considered essential to a successful and productive life in the UK and, as we have seen, form part of the requirement for passing the Life in the UK test in order to obtain British citizenship. There is plenty more about what exactly this required standard is later in this chapter.
- You must have sufficient knowledge of life in the UK – this again is part of the Life in the UK test. The material you have to study to pass this test is specially designed to give you the background knowledge you need.

If you fulfil all of these conditions, you will be eligible to start the process that, with the successful completion of the Citizenship Test, will lead to British citizenship.

Note

These are the general rules that apply, but the Home Office rules are extremely complex and everyone's situation is different. It is always essential that you check for detailed information and make sure that recent changes have not affected your case. Look for information on **www.ind.homeoffice.gov.uk** as this is the official source and will be the most up-to-date information.

Indefinite leave to remain

The conditions you must fulfil to apply for settlement (or indefinite leave to remain) and to take the test that you need to pass to be able to remain, will vary according to the grounds on which you are applying. The important point to remember is that you must make any application to stay before your existing permission to stay runs out. The requirements for English language skills and knowledge of life in the UK are the same as for those applying for citizenship.

Note

Your application for citizenship or indefinite leave to remain is discussed in greater detail in Chapter 9.

Again, it is essential to get up-to-date, detailed information and to check your own individual circumstances, so go to **www.ind.homeoffice.gov.uk**.

How good does your English need to be?

For some people, this will not be an issue. Many people come to Britain from other English-speaking countries or may have studied to a high level, so they will already have developed their language skills. However, if you cannot speak perfect English you may be worried about what standard of English you will need to reach in order to be eligible to become a British citizen.

The Government has stated that it is felt very important that every immigrant to the UK can speak, read and understand English. With the appropriate language skills everyone can live a more successful life and can play a fuller part in society. With good language skills many things become easier. Dealing with the world outside the family, whether in a social situation, or when dealing with officialdom, or shopping and going about everyday life, will be simpler and more straightforward as well as more pleasurable. Struggling with language means that many things are missed and the full benefit of any situation cannot be realised.

The level that the government has decided is necessary as a minimum requirement for people applying for naturalisation or indefinite leave to remain is that of ESOL Entry Level 3. ESOL stands for English for Speakers of Other Languages, i.e. it is for you if English is not your first language. As you would expect, if Entry Level 3 is the standard you must attain, there are two other entry levels before that and these are the ones that you may need to start with if you need to study to improve your language skills and bring them up to the required standard.

So, how do you know if your English needs to be improved? Maybe, as we said earlier, English is your first language or maybe you know that your standard is very high – you're fluent and never have any problem understanding others or making yourself understood. If so, you've no problem – you can apply to take your test as soon as you've studied and understood the material in Chapters 3, 4, 5, 6 and 7. But if you have a few problems or are simply unsure if you're up to the standard, then here are a few guidelines about the ESOL Entry Level 3.

At ESOL Entry Level 3, you should be able to:

• **Listen and answer**. You should be able to understand straightforward information that you are given and to follow simple explanations and instructions. You should be able to do all these things either face-to-face or over the telephone.

- **Speak sufficient English to be able to communicate.** This would include expressing your opinions and feelings or passing on information about topics with which you are familiar. Again, this could be either face-to-face or over the telephone. When speaking with someone you should be aware of the appropriate level of formality.
- **Hold a discussion about a familiar topic.** The aim of the discussion should be to reach a shared understanding with one or more people. You should be able to take your part in a discussion about a familiar topic, making your points and responding to points made by others.
- **Read and understand.** You should be able to read short, simple texts without help and understand the point of the text. You should also be able to obtain information from everyday sources such as a newspaper, a dictionary or a library.
- **Write to communicate.** This would include communicating information in, for example, letters or emails, or filling in forms in everyday life. Again, you should be aware of the different levels of formality that are possible in written communication and be able to choose the right one to fit the situation.

Top tip

If you are trying to improve your English, use everyday situations to help you. For example, you could use bus timetables, ask for directions in the street, initiate conversations with shop assistants. As you become aware of the opportunities for practice and improvement you will be helping yourself to become fluent.

Still in doubt?

If you still have some doubt as to whether your English will be of a high enough standard to enable to you take the test, you can get a quick assessment at your local learndirect centre. There are over 2000 learndirect centres in the UK so there should be one near you. If you need help to find one, ring their free helpline on 0800 101 901 or check out their website at **www.learndirect.co.uk**. Alternatively, you can telephone the Life in the UK Helpline on 0800 015 4245 or call into your local college of further education.

Advice in other languages

If you need advice on learning – including ESOL – it is available in a variety of other languages via these special learndirect helplines:

Farsi – tel. 0800 0931116
French – tel. 0800 093 1115
Gujarati – tel. 0800 093 1119
Punjabi – tel. 0800 093 1333
Polish – tel. 0800 093 1114
Somali – tel. 0800 093 1555
Sylheti – tel. 0800 093 1444
Urdu – tel. 0800 093 1118
Welsh – tel. 0800 100900

These helplines are free and available from 9.00 a.m. to 5.00 p.m., Monday to Friday

Exemptions from the English requirement

Exemptions from the language requirement may be made if it would be unreasonable to expect the applicant to fulfil it because of age or infirmity (physical or mental). The language requirement is normally waived when the applicant is aged 65 or over.

Exemptions for younger applicants are harder to come by. Exemption for under 65s will normally only be granted where the applicant:

- has a disability or long-term illness that severely restricts their mobility and their ability to attend language classes
- has a speech disability that limits their ability to have a conversation in English
- has a mental disability that stops them from learning another language.

How can you get your English up to the required standard?

If you do need help with your English and take a combined Citizenship and English Language Test, you will not need to find a test centre as this will all be organised as part of your course at the further education college, and they will be responsible for issuing the certificate (when you've passed, of course) that you will need to continue with your citizenship application.

If it is found that your standard of English is not of at least ESOL Entry Level 3, then don't worry – lessons are available. You will need to attend combined English language and citizenship classes. Most local further education or community colleges run these courses at reasonable prices and at various times, so check with your nearest college for full details. You will have to take a paper-based test to prove what English standard you have reached and will, if necessary, be able to work your way through the earlier levels until you reach the standard required to apply for naturalisation or indefinite leave to remain. Courses vary a lot, so do a little research to find the right course for you. Consider:

- **Cost** – they can cost from a few pounds to enormous amounts, so be sure to ask what the total cost will be.
- **Duration** – courses may run for a few weeks or for months. It is likely that the longer the course, the more emphasis will be put on the citizenship materials and you are more likely to be ready to take the test when you have finished the course.
- **Starting dates** – find one that is right for you. Some courses may have a 'rolling start', which means that you can join at any time rather than waiting for the start of a new session or term.

If you know that your English is not good enough to allow you to take the test right away, don't worry and do not let it put you off. If you intend to stay in the UK it is well worth the effort of improving your English as not only will it mean that you can pass your Life in the UK Test but it will also enhance your life. Life is much easier and more enjoyable if you can understand what is going on around you and you can take your place in society with pride.

Applying to take the test

Booking a British Citizenship Test is easy. First you need to find a test centre where you would like to sit the test. There are more than 90 test centres in the UK and they are usually in learning centres. You can find your nearest centre by visiting the website www.lifeintheuktest.gov.uk and clicking on the 'Find a test centre' section on the left-hand side of the home page. Alternatively, you can call the Life in the UK helpline on 0800 015 4245 and ask for the telephone number of your local test centre. You then simply contact your chosen test centre – either by telephone or in person – and book your test appointment. You will be offered a place in one of the test sessions taking place within one to four weeks of your request. There is a minimum waiting period of seven days between making your booking and being able to take the test. All the test centres have testing sessions at different times, so ask about this when you make your booking.

If, after you have made your booking, you find you need to cancel or change it, ring or call in at your test centre. If you are unable to give at least seven days notice of a change or cancellation, the test centre may charge you an administration fee – approximately £10.

At the test centre

When you arrive for your test appointment you will be asked for photographic ID to confirm your identity, and the test supervisor will record a few personal details such as your date of birth and postcode, so it is helpful to take some paperwork with you to confirm these details. Examples of acceptable photographic ID that you should take with you are:

- a passport
- a passport-sized photograph of yourself, endorsed (signed) by a professional person recognised by the UK Passport Agency (go to **www.ukpa.gov.uk/passport_countersign.asp** for more details of who would be acceptable to countersign your photo)
- a UK photo-card driving licence
- a Convention Travel Document (CTD) from the Home Office
- a Stateless Person Document (SPD) from the Home Office
- a Certificate of Identity Document (CID) from the Home Office
- an Immigration Status Document – this must contain a UK Residence Permit and include a photo of yourself.

A photo ID is essential – you will not be allowed to sit the test if you cannot produce satisfactory evidence of your identity. So, if you have any doubts about the validity of the document you intend to take, or problems in obtaining something acceptable, check before you attend the test centre.

At this point you will also be required to pay for your test – it currently costs £34 and most test centres will accept a variety of payment methods – you could check this at the time of making your booking so that you are prepared when you attend the test centre.

Using a computer during your test

Everyone has to use a computer to sit the British Citizenship Test, as the tests are all conducted online. Don't worry if you are not familiar with computers as there is help available on the Life in the UK Test website. There is a special section for people new to computers with very clear, step-by-step instructions on using a mouse and a keyboard. To get some practice in before the day of your test, you will be able to gain access to a computer either at your local college or library, where there are always people to help get you started. Take a note of the website address – www.lifeintheuktest.gov.uk – with you and overcome those fears!

If you have a particular condition that will hinder your use of a computer – visual impairment, for example – there is help available too. The program that operates the test can be set to read the questions out loud to you.

The test itself

The test itself, lasting 45 minutes, consists of 24 questions (chosen at random from a bank of approximately 400 questions) based on the material about life in the UK in the book produced by the Home Office (*Life in the United Kingdom – A Journey to Citizenship*). This is the material reproduced in the next five chapters in this book. All the answers to the test questions are to be found in those five chapters. Your answers will need to be indicated in one of four ways as the questions come in four different types (and the way that you need to do it will always be stated in the question):

1 You will select your answer from four options given. This is known as a 'multiple choice' question.

2 You will decide whether a given statement is true or false.

3 You will be given four options and must select two of them. If you try to answer with one option or three or four, your answer will not be correct – you must select the correct number of options.

4 You will be given two statements and you must decide which of these is correct.

Before you sit the actual test, the computer will give you the option to sit a practice test and it is always useful to do this to help you to settle down and to get comfortable with answering questions on a computer. Don't forget that you will not be able to consult any materials or notes during the actual test or the practice session. However, there will be plenty of time to try to recall the information you need to answer the questions and you will be able to go back to any questions that you have missed or are unsure about. The computer indicates those you have given an answer to and those you haven't, so it's easy to reconsider your answer or go back to questions that you have found difficult. Just remember that there is no need to rush. To pass the test you must get at least 18 of the 24 test questions correct (i.e. a minimum of 75% right) so bear this in mind when you're testing yourself.

When your test is finished, the test supervisor will inform you on the day whether you have passed or failed. Almost three quarters of the people who sit the test pass it. If you have passed you will be given a Pass Notification Letter. This is a very important piece of paper as you will need to include it as part of your application for citizenship or indefinite leave to remain, and it is not possible to get another one without sitting the test again, so keep it in a very safe place.

If you have failed, don't worry – you can sit the test as many times as you need, although you will have to book appointments and pay for each test that you take. Until you have passed the test, you cannot apply for citizenship.

Frequently asked questions

1 What happens if I repeatedly fail the test?
You will need to continue to study and wait until your knowledge of life in the UK, as set out in the official material, is at the required level before trying again. You may also want to check that your English is up to the required standard of ESOL Entry Level 3, as this could be a factor in your performance. Go

to the Knowledge of Life in the UK Test website (**www.lifeintheuktest.gov.uk**), which includes a short tutorial to help you prepare for the test and assess if you are ready to sit the test. If, after the extra preparation, you still find that you cannot pass the test, you may want to think about taking an ESOL with citizenship course or private tuition to help you prepare.

2 How can I take the test if I am visually impaired?

The computer can read out each question if required, and in some cases it will be possible for someone to help you enter your answers on the computer. Test centres can also provide support for people with special needs. Check this with the test centre you will be attending.

3 Why does someone whose first language is English, or who has lived and been educated here, have to meet the requirement?

The requirement is that all applicants must have knowledge of both the English language and of life in the UK. The Life in the UK Test gives those applicants who are already fluent English speakers a straightforward way to demonstrate that they also meet the knowledge of life in the UK requirements.

4 Some of the words and ideas in the official material are unfamiliar to me. Is there anywhere I can get help?

There is a handy glossary at the end of this book that will explain some of the words and ideas that you need to understand. It will also be helpful if you keep a dictionary beside you while you are studying the material.

5 Do European Union nationals need to take the test?

No. The provisions of the European Charter concerning free movement of labour mean that the British Government cannot impose a test such as this on nationals of the EU. However, the government encourages EU nationals to read the Life in the UK handbook, and/or to undertake language courses if they need to, so that they can lead full and active lives here. EU nationals will, however, have to meet the knowledge of life and language requirements if they go on to apply for naturalisation as a British citizen.

6 If I pass the ESOL course/test, will there be a time limit or will the pass last indefinitely?

A pass in either the knowledge of life test or an ESOL with citizenship course is not time-limited, so it will remain valid indefinitely. You can use the result to help you meet the requirements for both citizenship and indefinite leave to remain.

7. What should I do if I can't pass a Life in the UK Test or ESOL course before my leave to remain expires?

If your leave is due to expire before you can obtain the necessary evidence, you should apply to the Immigration and Nationality Directorate to extend your leave to remain. Failure to do so will mean that you are in the UK illegally and may be subject to removal. To find out how to extend your leave to remain you should either contact INEB on 0870 606 7766, or go to the website at www.homeoffice.gov.uk.

8. Will my dependants have to meet the requirement?

If your dependants are aged 18–65 they will also need to meet the requirement, unless they fall into one of the exempt categories (i.e. physical or mental impairment).

9. What happens if my dependants don't meet the requirement but I do?

Your dependants should apply for further leave to remain. The Life in the UK Test is about qualifying for citizenship or indefinite leave to remain, not about remaining in the UK. No one will be asked to leave the UK just because they have not been able to pass this test.

10. What happens if my dependants meet the requirement but I don't?

A dependant partner over the age of 18 may take the Life in the UK Test and pass, but they will not qualify for settlement as a dependant just because of that. The main applicant must also qualify for indefinite leave to remain, in order for them to be granted the same leave as a dependant.

Summary

In this chapter we have looked at what you need to consider and to do before you take your British Citizenship Test. In particular, we have examined the legal requirements that you need to fulfil to make sure you are eligible to take the test and also how to assess whether or not your standard of English will be sufficient for the test. We then went on to look at how to book a test and also what would happen at the test centre, so that you can be as prepared as possible for this important part of your quest for citizenship or indefinite leave to remain.

03 a changing society (from Life in the UK)

In this chapter you will:
- begin studying the official material you need to pass the test
- learn a little about the history of migration to the UK
- see how the lives of women, children and young people have changed in recent years.

Overview

All countries and societies change over time and this is especially true of Britain. This chapter looks at the various groups of people that have come to Britain recently and why they have migrated here. It also examines the changes in women's and children's lives that have taken place in the period since the Second World War, which ended in 1945.

As you read through this chapter you will realise that the face of British society has changed almost beyond recognition so that it is now a multicultural society, made up of many different nationalities, religions and cultures. You will also see how women's lives have changed and the effect this has had on children and young people and on society in general. As one section of society changes, so the rest of society must change to accommodate the new ways of working and thinking.

It is important that you pay particular attention to the many dates that are included in this first section of the official material, which involves much of the recent history of the UK. To help you, these have been listed in an easy-to-use timeline at the back of this book (see page 204).

Most of the material in the next five chapters has been reproduced from the official Home Office material and this is what you will be tested on. There is additional material included to further explain or enrich the information you have to learn. Two types of information box will be used.

This sort of box will contain additional information.

Note that you do not have to learn the facts enclosed in boxes like this in order to pass the test, but you may find things of interest or points that will help you to remember key facts.

You will also see boxes like this:

Check that you understand:

These boxes form part of the official material and are there to draw your attention to the things that you should have understood in the section just before the box. Go through the content of these boxes carefully. There is no guarantee that you will be asked questions on the subjects picked out in these boxes, but they should focus your attention on the most important parts of the official material you have just studied. If there is anything in these boxes that you do not understand, go back over the relevant sections.

Now on to the official information that comes from Chapter 2: A Changing Society, in the Home Office publication *Life in the United Kingdom – A Journey to Citizenship*.

* *

In this chapter there is information about:

Migration to Britain

- The long history of immigration to the United Kingdom
- Different reasons why people migrated to the UK
- Basic changes in immigration patterns over the last 30 years

The changing role of women

- Changes to family structures and women's rights since the 19th century
- Women's campaigns for rights, including the right to vote, in the late 19th and early 20th centuries
- Discrimination against women in the workplace and in education
- Changing attitudes to women working, and responsibilities of men and women in the home

Children, family and young people

- The identity, interests, tastes and lifestyle patterns of children and young people
- Education and work
- Health hazards: cigarettes, alcohol and illegal drugs
- Young people's political and social attitudes

Migration to Britain

Many people living in Britain today have their origins in other countries. They can trace their roots to regions throughout the world such as Europe, the Middle East, Africa, Asia and the Caribbean. In the distant past, invaders came to Britain, seized land and stayed. More recently, people come to Britain to find safety, jobs and a better life.

Britain is proud of its tradition of offering safety to people who are escaping persecution and hardship. For example, in the 16th and 18th centuries, Huguenots (French Protestants) came to Britain to escape religious persecution in France. In the mid-1840s there was a terrible famine in Ireland and many Irish people migrated to Britain. Many Irish men became labourers and helped to build canals and railways across Britain.

From 1880 to 1910, a large number of Jewish people came to Britain to escape racist attacks (called 'pogroms') in what was then called the Russian Empire and from the countries now called Poland, Ukraine and Belarus.

Migration since 1945

After the Second World War (1939–45), there was a huge task of rebuilding Britain. There were not enough people to do the work, so the British government encouraged workers from Ireland and other parts of Europe to come to the UK to help with the reconstruction. In 1948, people from the West Indies were also invited to come and work.

During the 1950s, there was still a shortage of labour in the UK. The UK encouraged immigration in the 1950s for economic reasons and many industries advertised for workers from overseas. For example, centres were set up in the West Indies to recruit people to drive buses. Textile and engineering firms from the north of England and the Midlands sent agents to India and Pakistan to find workers. For about 25 years, people from the West Indies, India, Pakistan, and later Bangladesh, travelled to work and settle in Britain.

The number of people migrating from these areas fell in the late 1960s because the government passed new laws to restrict immigration to Britain, although immigrants from 'old' Commonwealth countries such as Australia, New Zealand and Canada did not have to face such strict controls. During this time, however, Britain did admit 28,000 people of Indian origin who had been forced to leave Uganda and 22,000 refugees from South East Asia.

In the 1980s the largest immigrant groups came from the United States, Australia, South Africa, and New Zealand. In the early 1990s, groups of people from the former Soviet Union came to Britain looking for a new and safer way of life. Since 1994 there has been a global rise in mass migration for both political and economic reasons.

Check that you understand:
- Some of the historical reasons for immigration to the UK
- Some of the reasons for immigration to the UK since 1945
- The main immigrant groups coming to the UK since 1945, the countries they came from and kind of work they did

---

Test yourself

Now that you have studied this section, go to page 123 to find the practice questions that refer to this material and check that you have understood all the information.

If you have any problems with answering the questions about this section you should read through it again, paying particular attention to the areas pointed out in the 'Check that you understand' box.

The changing role of women

In 19th-century Britain, families were usually large and in many poorer homes men, women and children all contributed to the family income. Although they made an important economic contribution, women in Britain had fewer rights than men. Until 1857, a married woman had no right to divorce her husband. Until 1882, when a woman got married, her earnings, property and money automatically belonged to her husband.

In the late 19th and early 20th centuries, an increasing number of women campaigned and demonstrated for greater rights and, in particular, the right to vote. They became known as 'Suffragettes'. These protests decreased during the First World

War because women joined in the war effort and therefore did a much greater variety of work than they had before. When the First World War ended in 1918, women over the age of 30 were finally given the right to vote and to stand for election to Parliament. It was not until 1928 that women won the right to vote at 21, the same age as men.

Despite these improvements, women still faced discrimination in the workplace. For example, it was quite common for employers to ask women to leave their jobs when they got married. Many jobs were closed to women and it was difficult for women to enter universities. During the 1960s and 1970s there was increasing pressure from women for equal rights. Parliament passed new laws giving women the right to equal pay and prohibiting employers from discriminating against women because of their sex.

The Suffragettes

The political movement to get the vote for women – The Women's Social and Political Union, better known as the Suffragettes – was founded by Emmeline Pankhurst and her daughter Christabel at the start of the 20th century. They did not always keep to legal means to try to overcome the resistance and hostility they met and often protested with acts of violence and civil disobedience.

Women in Britain today

Women in Britain today make up 51% of the population, and 45% of the workforce. These days girls leave school, on average, with better qualifications than boys and there are now more women than men at university.

Employment opportunities for women are now much greater than they were in the past. Although women continue to be employed in traditionally female areas, such as healthcare, teaching, secretarial and retail work, there is strong evidence that attitudes are changing, and women are now active in a much wider range of work than before. Research shows that very few people today believe that women in Britain should stay at home and not go out to work. Today, almost three-quarters of women with school-age children are in paid work.

In most households, women continue to have the main responsibility for childcare and housework. There is evidence that there is now greater equality in homes and that more men are taking some responsibility for raising the family and doing housework. Despite this progress, many people believe that more needs to be done to achieve greater equality for women. There are still examples of discrimination against women, particularly in the workplace, despite the laws that exist to prevent it. Women still do not always have the same access to promotion and better-paid jobs. The average hourly pay rate for women is 20% less than for men, and after leaving university most women still earn less than men.

Check that you understand:
- When women aged over 30 were first given the right to vote
- When women were given equal voting rights with men
- Some of the important developments to create equal rights in the workplace

Test yourself

Now that you have studied this section, go to page 125 to find the practice questions that refer to this material and check that you have understood all the information.

If you have any problems with answering the questions about this section you should read through it again, paying particular attention to the areas pointed out in the 'Check that you understand' box.

Children, family and young people

In the UK there are almost 15 million children and young people up to the age of 19. This is almost one-quarter of the UK population.

Teenagers

Until the late 1950s and early 1960s young people dressed in the same way as their parents, listened to the same music and lived their lives in the same way. Then teenagers were invented – the word teenagers was brought into use at this time – and suddenly, with the advent of the contraceptive pill, pop music from artists such as The Beatles and The Rolling Stones, teenagers had much more freedom and started to live a different life. Fashion followed and young people soon began to look and behave in a totally different way from their parents.

Over the last 20 years, family patterns in Britain have been transformed because of changing attitudes towards divorce and separation. Today, 65% of children live with both birth parents, almost 25% live in lone-parent families, and 10% live within a stepfamily. Most children in Britain receive weekly pocket money from their parents and many get extra money for doing jobs around the house.

More information

Divorces are very common in the UK, with over 140,000 divorces in 2005, but the numbers are falling slightly – there were over 150,000 in 2004.

Children in the UK do not play outside the home as much as they did in the past. Part of the reason for this is increased home entertainment such as television, videos and computers. There is also increased concern for children's safety and there are many stories in newspapers about child molestation by strangers, but there is no evidence that this kind of danger is increasing.

More information

In Britain we watch more television than any other nation in Europe, and by the time a child is six he or she will have spent a year of their life in front of the television.

It is suspected that watching a lot of television can lead to health problems such as obesity and heart disease.

Source: NHS Direct

Young people have different identities, interests and fashions to older people. Many young people move away from their family home when they become adults but this varies from one community to another.

Education

The law states that children between the ages of 5 and 16 must attend school. The tests that pupils take are very important, and in England and Scotland children take national tests in English, mathematics and science when they are 7, 11 and 14 years old. (In Wales, teachers assess children's progress when they are 7 and 11 and they take a national test at the age of 14). The tests give important information about children's progress and achievement, the subjects they are doing well in and the areas where they need extra help.

Most young people take the General Certificate of Secondary Education (GCSE), or, in Scotland, Scottish Qualifications Authority (SQA) Standard Grade examinations when they are 16. At 17 and 18, many take vocational qualifications, General Certificates of Education at an Advanced level (AGCEs), AS level units or Higher/Advanced Higher Grades in Scotland. Schools and colleges will expect good GCSE or SQA Standard Grade results before allowing a student to enrol on an AGCE or Scottish Higher/Advanced Higher course.

AS levels are Advanced Subsidiary qualifications gained by completing three AS units. Three AS units are considered one-half of an AGCE. In the second part of the course, three more AS units can be studied to complete the AGCE qualification.

Many people refer to AGCEs by the old name of A levels. AGCEs are the traditional route for entry to higher education courses, but many higher education students enter with different kinds of qualifications.

One in three young people now go on to higher education at college or university. Some young people defer their university entrance for a year and take a 'gap year'. This year out of education often includes voluntary work and travel overseas. Some young people work to earn and save money to pay for their university fees and living expenses.

People over 16 years of age may also choose to study at Colleges of Further Education or Adult Education Centres. There is a wide range of academic and vocational courses available as well as courses which develop leisure interests and skills. Contact your local college for details.

Work

It is now common for young people to have a part-time job while they are still at school. It is thought there are 2 million children at work at any one time. The most common jobs are newspaper delivery and work in supermarkets and newsagents. Many parents believe that part-time work helps children to become more independent, as well as providing them (and sometimes their family) with extra income.

There are laws about the age when children can take up paid work (usually not before 14), the type of work they can do and the number of hours they can work (see **www.worksmart.org.uk** for more information).

It is very important to note that there are concerns for the safety of children who work illegally or who are not properly supervised and the employment of children is strictly controlled by law.

Child employment licences

Local councils operate a system of licensing for young people under the compulsory school age (i.e. usually until shortly after they reach the age of 16). This is to protect them from exploitation and dangerous working practices. Employers of young people must apply for a licence and ensure that the child's parents sign the appropriate forms.

Health hazards

Many parents in Britain worry that their children may misuse drugs and addictive substances.

Smoking:

Although cigarette smoking has fallen in the adult population, more young people are smoking, and more girls smoke than boys. By law, it is illegal to sell tobacco products to anyone under 16 years old. In some areas, smoking in public buildings and work environments is not allowed.

More information

A smoking ban will come into force in July 2007 that will make smoking in enclosed public places illegal in England.

This will affect factories and offices, pubs and shops, but will not affect private homes or smoking outdoors.

This follows similar bans in Northern Ireland, Scotland and Wales.

Alcohol:

Young people under the age of 18 are not allowed to buy alcohol in Britain but there is concern about the age some young people start drinking alcohol and the amount of alcohol they drink at one time, known as 'binge drinking'. It is illegal to be drunk in public and there are now more penalties to help control this problem, including on-the-spot fines.

Illegal drugs:

As in most countries it is an offence to possess drugs such as heroin, cocaine, ecstasy, amphetamines, and cannabis. Current statistics show that half of young adults, and about a third of the population as a whole, have used illegal drugs at one time or another.

There is a strong link between the use of hard drugs (e.g. crack cocaine and heroin) and crime, and also hard drugs and mental illness. The misuse of drugs has a huge social and financial cost for the country. This is a serious issue and British society needs to find an effective way of dealing with the problem.

Check that you understand
- The proportion of all young people who go on to higher education
- Lifestyle patterns of children and young people (e.g. pocket money, leaving home on reaching adulthood)
- Changing family patterns and attitudes to changing family patterns (e.g. divorce)
- That education in Britain is free and compulsory, and that there is compulsory testing (in England and Scotland) at ages 7, 11 and 14; there are also GCSE and/or vocational exams at 16; and Advanced level exams (A and AS) at ages 17 and 18
- That there is a government target that half of all young people attend higher education

- That there are strict laws regarding the employment of children
- That there are important health concerns and laws relating to children and young people and smoking, alcohol and drugs
- That young people are eligible to vote in elections from age 18

Young people's political and social attitudes

Young people in Britain can vote in elections from the age of 18. In the 2001 general election, however, only one in five first-time voters used their vote. There has been a great debate over the reasons for this. Some researchers think that that one reason is that young people are not interested in the political process.

More information

The voting age was reduced to 18 in 1969 and some people today would like to see this reduced still further – to 16.

Although most young people show little interest in party politics, there is strong evidence that many are interested in some specific political issues such as the environment and cruelty to animals.

In 2003 a survey of the attitudes of young people in England and Wales showed that they believe the five most important issues in Britain were crime, drugs, war/terrorism, racism and health. The same survey asked young people about their participation in political and community events. They found that 86% of young people had taken part in some form of community event over the past year and 50% had taken part in fund-raising or collecting money for charity. Similar results have been found in surveys in Scotland and Northern Ireland. Many children first get involved in these activities while at school where they study citizenship as part of the National Curriculum.

Check that you understand the key terms and vocabulary for this chapter

Migration to Britain:

- migrate, immigrate, immigration, immigrant
- persecution, famine, conflict

- labour, labourer
- recruit
- restrict
- political asylum
- the war effort

Changing role of women:
- income, earnings
- rights, equal rights
- campaign, demonstrate
- discriminate, discrimination
- prohibit
- workforce
- household
- promotion

Children, family and young people:
- eligible
- concern
- molestation
- attitudes
- hazards
- birth parent, stepfamily
- compulsory
- informal
- methods of assessment
- defer
- gap year
- independent
- income
- misuse
- addictive substances
- abuse
- binge drinking
- on-the-spot fines
- controlled drugs
- criminal offence
- possess
- heroin, cocaine, crack cocaine, ecstasy, amphetamines, cannabis

- burglary, mugging
- debate
- politicians, political process, party politics, political issues
- specific
- concern
- environment
- terrorism, racism
- participation
- fund-raising

Top tip

If there are words here that you do not understand (and unless English is your first language, there probably will be) do not avoid or ignore them.

Get hold of a dictionary (or use an online version) and look them up as this will make the whole process much easier. You can buy small dictionaries at very reasonable prices at some of the bargain bookstores that you will see in shopping centres. Or invest in a good one that will last you forever.

Test yourself

Now that you have studied this section, go to page 127 to find the practice questions that refer to this material and check that you have understood all the information.

If you have any problems with answering the questions about this section you should read through it again, paying particular attention to the areas pointed out in the 'Check that you understand' boxes.

✳✳✳

Summary

In this first section of official material we have looked at how UK society has changed over recent years and at the impact of those changes. You should pay particular attention to the historical background of immigration and the changes to women's voting rights.

You should also note how changing family patterns and attitudes are having an impact on family life, working life and society as a whole.

Don't forget to test yourself as you go along – master one section of material before you tackle another and also use the glossary at the back of the book, which will help you with any unfamiliar words.

04

UK today: a profile (from Life in the UK)

In this chapter you will:
- learn about British society today
- look at how and why celebrations take place in Britain
- see the regional differences in Britain's population.

Overview

This is the second of five chapters that form the material supplied by the Home Office that you need to learn to pass the test. There are a lot of statistics and dates for you to learn in this chapter, so you will need to take special note of all these details. To help you with remembering the dates there is a handy reference box at the end of the chapter.

This chapter gives you lots of information about who lives in Britain today. There are many figures given about the UK population taken from the 2001 census, so it is important that you study this section carefully. There is also information about the regional differences that you will find in the UK. This is followed by a section about customs and traditions and this is where you will need to memorise the dates of the various festivals celebrated in the UK.

Now on to the official information that comes from Chapter 3: UK Today: A Profile, in the Home Office publication *Life in the United Kingdom – A Journey to Citizenship*.

✳✳✳

In this chapter there is information about:

- The population of the UK
- The census
- Ethnic diversity
- The regions of Britain
- Religions and religious freedom
- Customs and traditions

Population

In 2005, the population of the United Kingdom was recorded at just under 60 million people.

UK population 2005

England	(84% of the population)	50.1 million
Scotland	(8% of the population)	5.1 million
Wales	(5% of the population)	2.9 million
N. Ireland	(3% of the population)	1.7 million
Total UK		59.8 million

Source: National Statistics

The population has grown by 7.7% since 1971, and growth has been faster in more recent years. Although the general population in the UK has increased in the last 20 years, in some areas such as the North-East and North-West of England there has been a decline.

Both the birth rate and the death rate are falling and as a result the UK now has an ageing population. For instance, there are more people over 60 than children under 16. There is also a record number of people aged 85 and over.

The census

A census is a count of the whole population. It also collects statistics on topics such as age, place of birth, occupation, ethnicity, housing, health and marital status.

A census has been taken every ten years since 1801, except during the Second World War. The next census will take place in 2011.

During a census, a form is delivered to every household in the country. This form asks for detailed information about each member of the household and must be completed by law. The information remains confidential and anonymous; it can only be released to the public after 100 years, when many people researching their family history find it very useful. General census information is used to identify population trends and to help planning. More information about the census, the census form and statistics from previous censuses can be found at **www.statistics.gov.uk/census**.

More information

Many people research their family histories using censuses, and it has now become a popular hobby in the UK.

If you would like to make a start on researching your family's history, a useful book is *Teach Yourself Tracing Your Family History* by Stella Colwell.

Ethnic diversity

The UK population is ethnically diverse and is changing rapidly, especially in large cities such as London, so it is not always easy to get an exact picture of the ethnic origin of all the population from census statistics. Each of the four countries of the UK (England, Wales, Scotland and Northern Ireland) has different customs, attitudes and histories.

People of Indian, Pakistani, Chinese, Black Caribbean, Black African, Bangladeshi and mixed ethnic descent make up 8.3% of the UK population. Today about half of the members of these communities were born in the United Kingdom.

There are also considerable numbers of people resident in the UK who are of Irish, Italian, Greek and Turkish Cypriot, Polish, Australian, Canadian, New Zealand and American descent. Large numbers have also arrived since 2004 from the new East European member states of the European Union. These groups are not identified separately in the census statistics in the following table.

UK Population 2001	Million	UK population %
White (including people of European, Australian, American descent)	54.2	92
Mixed	0.7	1.2
Asian or Asian British		
Indian	1.1	1.8
Pakistani	0.7	1.3
Bangladeshi	0.3	0.5
Other Asian	0.2	0.4
Black or Black British		
Black Caribbean	0.6	1.0
Black African	0.5	0.8
Black Other	0.1	0.2
Chinese	0.2	0.4
Other	0.2	0.4

Source: National Statistics from the 2001 census

Where do the largest ethnic minority groups live?

The figures from the 2001 census show that most members of ethnic minority groups in the UK live in England, where they make up 9% of the total population. 45% of all ethnic minority people live in the London area, where they form nearly one-third of the population (29%). Other areas of England with large ethnic minority populations are the West Midlands, the South East, the North West, and Yorkshire and Humberside.

Proportion of ethnic minority groups in the countries of the UK

England	9%	Wales	2%
Scotland	2%	Northern Ireland	less than 1%

The nations and regions of the UK

The UK is a medium-sized country. The longest distance on the mainland, from John O'Groats on the north coast of Scotland to Land's End in the south-west corner of England, is about 870 miles (approximately 1,400 kilometres). Most of the population live in towns and cities.

More information

The furthest that anyone can live from the sea in the UK is approximately 75 miles (120 km).

There are many variations in culture and language in the different parts of the United Kingdom. This is seen in differences in architecture, in some local customs, in types of food, and especially in language. The English language has many accents and dialects. These are a clear indication of regional differences in the UK. Well-known dialects in England are Geordie (Tyneside), Scouse (Liverpool) and Cockney (London). Many other languages in addition to English are spoken in the UK, especially in multicultural cities.

In Wales, Scotland and Northern Ireland, people speak different varieties and dialects of English. In Wales, too, an increasing number of people speak Welsh, which is taught in schools and universities. In Scotland Gaelic is spoken in some parts of the Highlands and Islands and in Northern Ireland a few people speak Irish Gaelic. Some of the dialects of English spoken in

Scotland show the influence of the old Scottish language, Scots. One of the dialects spoken in Northern Ireland is called Ulster Scots.

Check that you understand:

- The size of the current UK population
- The population of Scotland, Wales and Northern Ireland
- What the census is and when the next one will be
- What the largest ethnic minorities in the UK are
- Where most ethnic minority people live
- What languages other than English are spoken in Wales, Scotland and Northern Ireland
- Some of the ways you can identify regional differences in the UK

Test yourself

Now that you have studied this section, go to page 130 to find the practice questions that refer to this material and check that you have understood all the information.

If you have any problems with answering the questions about this section you should read through it again, paying particular attention to the areas pointed out in the 'Check that you understand' box.

Religion

Although the UK is historically a Christian society, everyone has the right to practise the religion of their choice. In the 2001 census, just over 75% said they had a religion; 7 out of 10 of these were Christians. There were also a considerable number of people who followed other religions. Although many people in the UK said they held religious beliefs, currently only around 10% of the population attend religious services. More people attend services in Scotland and Northern Ireland than in England and Wales. In London the number of people who attend religious services is increasing.

Religions in the UK	%
Christian (10% of whom are Roman Catholic)	71.6
Muslim	2.7
Hindu	1.0
Sikh	0.6
Jewish	0.5
Buddhist	0.3
Other	0.3
Total all	77
No religion	15.5
Not stated	7.3

Source: National Statistics from the 2001 census

The Christian Churches

In England there is a constitutional link between church and state. The official church of the state is the Church of England. The Church of England is called the Anglican Church in other countries and the Episcopal Church in Scotland and in the USA. The Church of England is a Protestant church and has existed since the Reformation in the 1530s. The king or queen (the monarch) is the head, or Supreme Governor, of the Church of England. The monarch is not allowed to marry anyone who is not Protestant. The spiritual leader of the Church of England is the Archbishop of Canterbury. The monarch has the right to select the Archbishop and other senior church officials, but usually the choice is made by the Prime Minister and a committee appointed by the Church. Several Church of England bishops sit in the House of Lords. In Scotland, the established church is the Presbyterian Church; its head is the Chief Moderator. There is no established church in Wales or in Northern Ireland.

Other Protestant Christian groups in the UK are Baptists, Presbyterians, Methodists and Quakers. 10% of Christians are Roman Catholic (40% in Northern Ireland).

Patron saints

England, Scotland Wales and Northern Ireland each have a national saint called a patron saint. Each saint has a feast day. In the past these were celebrated as holy days when many people had a day off work. Today these are not public holidays except for 17 March in Northern Ireland.

Patron saints' days

St. David's day, Wales	1 March
St. Patrick's day, Northern Ireland	17 March
St. George's day, England	23 April
St. Andrew's day, Scotland	30 November

There are also four public holidays a year called Bank Holidays. These are of no religious or national significance.

More information

The four Bank Holidays are:

New Year's Day – taken on the 1 January
May Day – taken on the first Monday in May
Spring Holiday – taken on the last Monday in May
Summer Holiday – taken on the last Monday in August

Check that you understand:

- The percentage (%) of the UK population who say they are Christian
- How many people say they have no religion
- What percentage are Muslim, Hindu, Sikh, Jewish, Buddhist
- Everyone in the UK has the right to practise their religion
- The Anglican Church, or Church of England, is the church of the state in England (established church)
- The monarch (king or queen) is head of the Church of England
- In Scotland the established church is the Presbyterian Church of Scotland. In Wales and Northern Ireland there is no established church.

Test yourself

Now that you have studied this section, go to page 133 to find the practice questions that refer to this material and check that you have understood all the information.

If you have any problems with answering the questions about this section you should read through it again, paying particular attention to the areas pointed out in the 'Check that you understand' box.

Customs and traditions

Festivals

Throughout the year there are festivals of art, music and culture, such as the Notting Hill Carnival in west London and the Edinburgh Festival. Customs and traditions from various religions, such as Eid ul-Fitr (Muslim), Diwali (Hindu) and Hanukkah (Jewish) are widely recognised in the UK. Children learn about these at school. The main Christian festivals are Christmas and Easter. There are also celebrations of non-religious traditions such as New Year.

The main Christian festivals

Christmas Day

25 December, celebrates the birth of Jesus Christ. It is a public holiday. Many Christians go to church on Christmas Eve (24 December) or on Christmas Day itself. Christmas is also usually celebrated by people who are not Christian. People usually spend the day at home and eat a special meal, which often includes turkey. They give each other gifts, send each other cards and decorate their houses. Many people decorate a tree. Christmas is a special time for children. Very young children believe that an old man, Father Christmas (or Santa Claus), brings them presents during the night. He is always shown in pictures with a long white beard, dressed in red. Boxing Day, 26 December, is the day after Christmas. It is a public holiday.

More information

The other major Christian festival celebrated in the UK is Easter. It marks the resurrection of Jesus Christ, three days after he was crucified.

Easter can be on any date between March 22 and April 25. The date is calculated as being the first Sunday after the first full moon after the vernal equinox (the day in spring when day and night are of equal length).

Other festivals and traditions

New Year
1 January, is a public holiday. People usually celebrate on the night of 31 December. In Scotland, 31 December is called Hogmanay and 2 January is a public holiday. In Scotland Hogmanay is a bigger holiday for some people than Christmas.

Valentine's Day
14 February, is when lovers exchange cards and gifts. Sometimes people send anonymous cards to someone they secretly admire.

April Fool's Day
1 April, is a day when people play jokes on each other until midday. Often TV and newspapers carry stories intended to deceive credulous viewers and readers.

More information

One of the most famous April Fool's jokes played on TV was played in 1957 by the BBC when they broadcast a 'documentary' that showed spaghetti being grown on trees in Switzerland!

Mother's Day
The Sunday three weeks before Easter is a day when children send cards or buy gifts for their mothers. Easter is also an important Christian festival.

Hallowe'en
31 October, is a very ancient festival. Young people will often dress up in frightening costumes to play 'trick or treat'. Giving

them sweets or chocolates might stop them playing a trick on you. Sometimes people carry lanterns made out of pumpkins with a candle inside.

Guy Fawkes Night

5 November, is an occasion when people in Great Britain set off fireworks at home or in special displays. The origin of this celebration was an event in 1605, when a group of Catholics led by Guy Fawkes failed in their plan to kill the Protestant king with a bomb in the Houses of Parliament.

Remembrance Day

11 November, commemorates those who died fighting in World War 1, World War 2 and other wars. Many people wear poppies (a red flower) in memory of those who died. At 11 a.m. there is a two-minute silence.

Dates to remember

14 February	St. Valentine's Day
1 March	St. David's Day (national day of Wales)
17 March	St. Patrick's Day (national day of Ireland)
1 April	April Fools' Day
23 April	St. George's Day (national day of England)
30 November	St. Andrew's Day (national day of Scotland)
5 November	Guy Fawkes Night (also known as Bonfire Night)
11 November	Remembrance Day
25 December	Christmas Day
26 December	Boxing Day

Sport

Sport of all kinds plays a major part in many people's lives. Football, tennis, rugby, and cricket are very popular sports in the UK. There are no United Kingdom teams for football and rugby. England, Scotland, Wales and Northern Ireland have their own teams. Important sporting events include, the Grand National horse race, the Football Association (FA) cup final (and equivalents in Northern Ireland, Scotland and Wales), the Open golf championship and the Wimbledon tennis tournament.

Sporting occasions

Many large sporting events are held on approximately the same date each year. These events are well attended and also watched by millions on television. Here are a few examples:

Grand National (horse race)	April
Wimbledon (tennis)	June/July
The University Boat Race	April
The FA Cup Final	May
Six Nations rugby competition	February/March
Cheltenham Gold Cup (horse racing festival)	March
Henley Regatta (sailing)	July
Cowes Week (sailing)	August
Royal Ascot (horse racing meeting)	June
Epsom Derby	June

Check that you understand:

- Which sports are most popular in the UK
- The patron saints' days in England, Scotland, Wales and Northern Ireland
- What Bank Holidays are
- The main traditional festivals in the UK
- That the main festivals in the UK are Christian based, but that important festivals from other religions are recognised and explained to children in schools

Test yourself

Now that you have studied this section, go to page 136 to find the practice questions that refer to this material and check that you have understood all the information.

If you have any problems with answering the questions about this section you should read through it again, paying particular attention to the areas pointed out in the 'Check that you understand' box.

✳ ✳

Summary

This section of the *Life in the UK* material has examined how the UK is today. There are lots of facts and figures in this chapter, especially concerning the way the population of the UK is made up of different ethnicities and religions, and you will need to make a special effort to understand and learn these figures in preparation for your test.

Much information is given about religious beliefs as detailed in the 2001 census.

There are also many dates included in the section on customs and traditions, detailing when the various celebrations that are described take place in the UK.

05

how the United Kingdom is governed (from Life in the UK)

In this chapter you will:

- learn about the government institutions in the UK
- find out about the devolved administrations
- see how the UK takes its place in Europe and the world.

Overview

This chapter from *Life in the UK* delves into how government in Britain works, and you should pay particular attention to the institutions that are examined in this chapter and how they work together to produce a fair and efficient system.

The chapter covers Parliament and how the political party system affects the way Britain is governed; it goes on to explain how the formal institutions, such as the monarchy and the House of Commons, affect people's lives at a national and local level. It then looks at local government and, on a wider scale, how power has been devolved to Scotland, Wales and Northern Ireland.

Now on to the official information that comes from Chapter 4: How the UK is Governed, in the Home Office publication *Life in the United Kingdom – A Journey to Citizenship*.

* *

In this chapter there is information about:

Government

- The system of government
- The monarchy
- The electoral system
- Political Parties
- Being a citizen
- Voting
- Contacting your MP
- The UK in Europe and the world
- The European Union
- The Commonwealth
- The United Nations

The British Constitution

As a constitutional democracy, the United Kingdom is governed by a wide range of institutions, many of which provide checks on each other's powers. Most of these institutions are of long standing: they include the monarchy, Parliament, (consisting of the House of Commons and the House of Lords), the office of Prime Minister, the Cabinet, the judiciary, the police, the civil service, and the institutions of local government. More recently, devolved administrations have been set up for Scotland, Wales and Northern Ireland. Together, these formal institutions, laws and conventions form the British Constitution. Some people would argue that the roles of other less formal institutions, such as the media and pressure groups, should also be seen as part of the Constitution.

The British Constitution is not written down in any single document, as are the constitutions of many other countries. This is mainly because the United Kingdom has never had a lasting revolution, like America or France, so our most important institutions have been in existence for hundreds of years. Some people believe that there should be a single document, but others believe that an unwritten constitution allows more scope for institutions to adapt to meet changing circumstances and public expectations.

The monarchy

Queen Elizabeth II is the Head of State of the United Kingdom. She is also the monarch or Head of State for many countries in the Commonwealth. The UK, like Denmark, the Netherlands, Norway, Spain and Sweden, has a constitutional monarchy. This means that the king or queen does not rule the country, but appoints the government which the people have chosen in democratic elections. Although the king or queen can advise, warn and encourage the Prime Minister, the decisions on government policies are made by the Prime Minister and Cabinet.

The Queen has reigned since her father's death in 1952. Prince Charles, the Prince of Wales, her oldest son, is the heir to the throne.

The Queen has important ceremonial duties such as the opening of the new parliamentary session each year. On this occasion the Queen makes a speech that summarises the government's policies for the year ahead.

Government

The system of government in the United Kingdom is a parliamentary democracy. The UK is divided into 646 parliamentary constituencies and at least every five years voters in each constituency elect their Member of Parliament (MP) in a general election. All of the elected MPs form the House of

Commons. Most MPs belong to a political party, and the party with the largest number of MPs in the House of Commons forms the government.

The law that requires new elections to Parliament to be held at least every five years is so fundamental that no government has sought to change it. A Bill to change it is the only one to which the House of Lords must give its consent.

Some people argue that the power of Parliament is lessened because of the obligation on the United Kingdom to accept the rules of the European Union and the judgments of the European Court, but it was Parliament itself which created these obligations.

Calling an election

General elections are held at least every five years – this is the maximum the government can be in power before having to step down and see if the voters still want them. However, a Prime Minister can decide to hold an election at any time before this five-year period is finished if he or she thinks that their party has a good chance of winning – and having a further five years in power. Calling an election in this way is sometimes referred to as 'going to the country'.

The House of Commons

The House of Commons is the more important of the two chambers in Parliament, and its members are democratically elected. Nowadays the Prime Minister and almost all the members of the Cabinet are members of the House of Commons. The members of the House of Commons are called 'Members of Parliament' or MPs for short. Each MP represents a parliamentary constituency, or area of the country: there are 646 of these. MPs have a number of different responsibilities. They represent everyone in their constituency, they help to create new laws, they scrutinise and comment on what the government is doing, and they debate important national issues.

Elections

There must be a general election to elect MPs at least every five years, though they may be held sooner if the Prime Minister so decides. If an MP dies or resigns, there will be another election, called a by-election, in his or her constituency. MPs are elected through a system called 'first past the post'. In each constituency, the candidate who gets the most votes is elected. The government is then formed by the party which wins the majority of constituencies.

By-elections

The 'turn out' – the number of people voting – at by-elections is usually substantially less than the turn out at general elections. There is less interest and less publicity surrounding a by-election as the result will not change which political party governs the country.

The Whips

The Whips are a small group of MPs appointed by their party leaders. They are responsible for discipline in their party and making sure MPs attend the House of Commons to vote. The Chief Whip often attends Cabinet or Shadow Cabinet meetings and arranges the schedule of proceedings in the House of Commons with the Speaker.

The Whip system

In the House of Commons, the party Whips for the three main parties consist of the Chief Whip, a Deputy Chief Whip and a varying number of junior Whips. Each of the smaller opposition parties also normally has a Whip. Their job is to keep MPs informed of forthcoming business and to maintain the party's voting strength by ensuring MPs attend important debates and votes (this is particularly important if votes are expected to be close). They also play an important role by passing on to party leadership the opinions of backbench members.

European parliamentary elections

Elections for the European Parliament are also held every five years. There are 78 seats for representatives from the UK in the European Parliament and elected members are called Members of the European Parliament (MEPs). Elections to the European Parliament use a system of proportional representation, whereby seats are allocated to each party in proportion to the total votes it won.

The House of Lords

Members of the House of Lords, known as peers, are not elected and do not represent a constituency. The role and membership of the House of Lords have recently undergone big changes. Until 1958 all peers were either 'hereditary', meaning that their titles were inherited, senior judges, or bishops of the Church of England. Since 1958 the Prime Minister has had the power to appoint peers just for their own lifetime. These peers, known as Life Peers, have usually had a distinguished career in politics, business, law or some other profession. This means that debates in the House of Lords often draw on more specialist knowledge than is available to members of the House of Commons. Life Peers are appointed by the Queen on the advice of the Prime Minister, but they include people nominated by the leaders of the other main parties and by an independent Appointments Commission for non-party peers.

In the last few years the hereditary peers have lost the automatic right to attend the House of Lords, although they are allowed to elect a few of their number to represent them.

While the House of Lords is usually the less important of the two chambers of Parliament, it is more independent of the government. It can suggest amendments or propose new laws, which are then discussed by the House of Commons. The House of Lords can become very important if the majority of its members will not agree to pass a law for which the House of Commons has voted. The House of Commons has powers to overrule the House of Lords, but these are very rarely used.

The Prime Minister

The Prime Minister (PM) is the leader of the political party in power. He or she appoints the members of the Cabinet and has control over many important public appointments. The official home of the Prime Minister is 10 Downing Street, in central London, near the Houses of Parliament; he or she also has a country house not far from London called Chequers. The Prime Minister can be changed if the MPs in the governing party decide to do so, or if he or she wishes to resign. More usually, the Prime Minister resigns when his or her party is defeated in a general election.

The Cabinet

The Prime Minister appoints about 20 senior MPs to become
ministers in charge of departments. These include the
Chancellor of the Exchequer, responsible for the economy, the
Home Secretary, responsible for law, order and immigration, the
Foreign Secretary, and ministers (called 'Secretaries of State') for
education, health and defence. The Lord Chancellor, who is the
minister responsible for legal affairs, is also a member of the
Cabinet but sat in the House of Lords rather than the House of
Commons. Following legislation passed in 2005, it is now
possible for the Lord Chancellor to sit in the Commons. These
ministers form the Cabinet, a small committee which usually
meets weekly and makes important decisions about government
policy which often then have to be debated or approved by
Parliament.

The Opposition

The second largest party in the House of Commons is called the
Opposition. The Leader of the Opposition is the person who
hopes to become the Prime Minister if his or her party wins the
next general election. The Leader of the Opposition leads his or
her party in pointing out the government's failures and
weaknesses; one important opportunity to do this is at Prime
Minister's Questions which takes places every week while
Parliament is sitting. The Leader of the Opposition also
appoints senior opposition MPs to lead criticism of government
ministers, and together they form the Shadow Cabinet.

The role of the Opposition

The Opposition's role consists of three main aims:

- to contribute to the formulation of policy and legislation by constructive criticism
- to oppose government proposals it considers unacceptable and to seek amendments to government bills
- to use time in parliament and in the media to put forward its own policies in order to improve its chances of winning at the next general election.

The Speaker

Debates in the House of Commons are chaired by the Speaker, the chief officer of the House of Commons. The Speaker is politically neutral. He or she is an MP, elected by fellow MPs to keep order during political debates and to make sure the rules are followed. This includes making sure the Opposition has a guaranteed amount of time to debate issues it chooses. The Speaker also represents Parliament at ceremonial occasions.

The party system

Under the British system of parliamentary democracy, anyone can stand for election as an MP but they are unlikely to win an election unless they have been nominated to represent one of the major political parties. These are the Labour Party, the Conservative Party, the Liberal Democrats, or one of the parties representing Scottish, Welsh, or Northern Irish interests. There are just a few MPs who do not represent any of the main political parties and are called 'independents'. The main political parties actively seek members among ordinary voters to join their debates, contribute to their costs, and help at elections for Parliament or for local government; they have branches in most constituencies and they hold policy-making conferences every year.

More information

If you would like to read more about the political system of the UK, a good place to start would be the book *Teach Yourself Politics* by Peter Joyce.

Pressure and lobby groups

Pressure groups are organisations that try to influence government policy. They play a very important role in politics. There are many pressure groups in the UK. They may represent economic interests (such as the Confederation of British Industry, the Consumers' Association, or the trade unions) or views on particular subjects (e.g. Greenpeace or Liberty). The general public is more likely to support pressure groups than join a political party.

Why do we have pressure groups?

Pressure groups in British politics offer the public more democracy in addition to their right to vote in elections. They mean that the public can become involved in issues that interest or concern them.

The aim of pressure groups is to influence the people who have the power to make decisions on issues of concern.

Pressure groups are varied – they range from the CBI (Confederation of British Industry) to small groups trying to change local issues.

The civil service

Civil servants are managers and administrators who carry out government policy. They have to be politically neutral and professional, regardless of which political party is in power. Although civil servants have to follow the policies of the elected government, they can warn ministers if they think a policy is impractical or not in the public interest. Before a general election takes place, top civil servants study the Opposition party's politics closely in case they need to be ready to serve a new government with different aims and policies.

Devolved administration

In order to give people in Wales and Scotland more control of matters that directly affect them, in 1997 the government began a programme of devolving power from central government. Since 1999 there has been a Welsh Assembly, a Scottish Parliament, and, periodically, a Northern Ireland Assembly. Although policy and laws governing defence, foreign affairs, taxation, and social security all remain under central UK government control, many other public services now come under the control of devolved administrations in Wales and Scotland.

Both the Scottish Parliament and Welsh Assembly have been set up using forms of proportional representation which ensures that each party gets a number of seats in proportion to the number of votes they receive. Similarly, proportional representation is used in Northern Ireland in order to ensure 'power sharing' between the Unionist majority (mainly Protestant) and the substantial (mainly Catholic) minority aligned to Irish nationalist parties. A different form of proportional representation is used for elections to the European Parliament.

More information

Definition of devolution: transfer of authority from a central government to a regional government.

The Welsh Assembly Government

The National Assembly for Wales, or Welsh Assembly Government (WAG), is situated in Cardiff, the capital city of Wales. It has 60 Assembly Members (AMs) and elections are held every four years. Members can speak in either Welsh or English and all its publications are in both languages. The Assembly has the power to make decisions on important matters such as education policy, the environment, health services, transport and local government, and to pass laws for Wales on these matters within a statutory framework set out by the UK Parliament at Westminster.

The Parliament of Scotland

A long campaign in Scotland for more independence and democratic control led to the formation in 1999 of the Parliament of Scotland, which sits in Edinburgh, the capital city of Scotland.

There are 129 Members of the Scottish Parliament (MSPs) elected by a form of proportional representation. This has led to the sharing of power in Scotland between the Labour and

Liberal Democratic parties. The Scottish Parliament can pass legislation for Scotland on all matters that are not specifically reserved to the UK Parliament. The matters on which the Scottish Parliament can legislate include civil and criminal law, health, education, planning and the raising of additional taxes.

The Northern Ireland Assembly

A Northern Ireland Parliament was established in 1922 when Ireland was divided, but it was abolished in 1972 shortly after the Troubles broke out in 1969.

Soon after the end of the Troubles, the Northern Ireland Assembly was established with a power-sharing agreement which distributes ministerial offices among the main parties. The Assembly has 108 elected members known as MLAs (Members of the Legislative Assembly). Decision-making powers devolved to Northern Ireland include education, agriculture, the environment, health and social services in Northern Ireland.

The UK government kept the power to suspend the Northern Ireland Assembly if the political leaders no longer agreed to work together or if the Assembly was not working in the interests of the people of Northern Ireland. This has happened several times and the Assembly is currently suspended (2006). This means that the elected assembly members do not have the power to pass bills or make decisions.

Local government

Towns, cities, and rural areas in the UK are governed by democratically elected councils, often called local authorities. Some areas have both district and county councils which have different functions, although most larger towns and cities will have a single local authority. Many councils representing towns and cities appoint a mayor who is the ceremonial leader of the council but in some towns a mayor is appointed to be the effective leader of the administration. London has 33 local authorities, with the Greater London Authority and the Mayor of London co-ordinating policies across the capital. Local authorities are required to provide 'mandatory services' in their area. These services include education, housing, social services, passenger transport, the fire service, rubbish collection, planning, environmental health and libraries.

Most of the money for the local authority services comes from the government through taxes. Only about 20% is funded locally through the collection of 'council tax' a local tax set by councils to help pay for local services. It applies to all domestic properties, including houses, bungalows, flats, maisonettes, mobile homes or houseboats, whether owned or rented. Elections for councillors are held in May each year. Many candidates stand for council election as members of a political party.

The judiciary

In the UK the laws made by Parliament are the highest authority. But often important questions arise about how the laws are to be interpreted in particular cases. It is the task of the judges (who are together called 'the judiciary') to interpret the law, and the government may not interfere with their role. Often the actions of the government are claimed to be illegal and, if the judges agree, then the government must either change its policies or ask Parliament to change the law. This has become all the more important in recent years, as the judges now have the task of applying the Human Rights Act. If they find that a public body is not respecting a person's human rights, they may order that body to change its practices and to pay compensation, if appropriate. If the judges believe that an Act of Parliament is incompatible with the Human Rights Act, they cannot change it themselves but they can ask Parliament to consider doing so.

Judges cannot, however, decide whether people are guilty or innocent of serious crimes. When someone is accused of a serious crime, a jury will decide whether he or she is innocent or guilty and, if guilty, the judges will decide on the penalty. For less important crimes, a magistrate will decide on guilt and on any penalty.

More information

Anyone between the ages of 18 and 70 who is on the electoral register can be called to serve on a jury and it is a very important civic duty. Approximately 450,000 people are called for jury service every year.

Trials are heard in a Crown Court by 12 jurors and a judge, and service usually lasts for up to two weeks. The cases heard by juries are the more serious ones such as those involving murder, fraud, burglary and serious assault.

The police

The police service is organised locally, with one force for each county or group of counties. The largest force is the Metropolitan Police, which serves London and is based at New Scotland Yard. Northern Ireland as a whole is served by the Police Service for Northern Ireland (PSNI). The police have 'operational independence', which means that the government cannot instruct them on what to do in any particular case. But the powers of the police are limited by law and their finances are controlled by the government and by police authorities made up of councillors and magistrates. The Independent Police Complaints Commission (or, in Northern Ireland, the Police Ombudsman) investigates serious complaints against the police.

Non-departmental public bodies (quangos)

Non-departmental public bodies, also known as quangos, are independent organisations that carry out functions on behalf of the public which it would be inappropriate to place under the political control of a Cabinet minister. There are many hundreds of these bodies, carrying out a wide variety of public duties. Appointments to these bodies are usually made by ministers, but they must do so in an open and fair way.

A few examples of non-departmental public bodies

Trading bodies set up by central government that raise revenue: Her Majesty's Stationery Office (official and semi-official publications), Forestry Commission, National Savings Bank

Spending agencies funded by government: Regional Health Authorities, Higher Education Funding Councils, Sports Council, Arts Council

Quasi-judicial and prosecuting bodies: Criminal Injuries Compensation Authority, Police Complaints Authority, Crown Prosecution Service

Statutory Advisory Bodies to Ministers: Health and Safety Commission, Law Commission, Commission for Racial Equality, Equal Opportunities Commission, Advisory Board on Naturalisation and Integration

Development agencies (many of which are public–private partnerships): Scottish Enterprise, Highlands and Islands Development Board (Scotland), Welsh Development Agency, Rural Development Commission

The role of the media

Proceedings in Parliament are broadcast on digital television and published in official reports such as Hansard, which is available in large libraries and on the internet: **www.parliament.uk**. Most people, however, get their information about political issues and events from newspapers (often called the press), television and radio.

The UK has a free press, meaning that what is written in newspapers is free from government control. Newspaper owners and editors hold strong political opinions and run campaigns to try and influence government policy and public opinion. As a result it is sometimes difficult to distinguish fact from opinion in newspaper coverage.

By law, radio and television coverage of the political parties at election periods must be balanced so equal time has to be given to rival viewpoints. But broadcasters are free to interview politicians in a tough and lively way.

Who can vote?

The UK has had a fully democratic system since 1928, when women were allowed to vote at 21, the same age as men. The present voting age of 18 was set in 1969, (and with a few exceptions such as convicted prisoners) all UK-born and naturalised citizens have full civic rights, including the right to vote and do jury service.

Citizens of the UK, the Commonwealth and the Irish Republic (if resident in the UK) can vote in all public elections. Citizens of EU states who are resident in the UK can vote in all elections except national parliamentary (general) elections.

In order to vote in a parliamentary, local or European election, you must have your name on the register of electors, known as the electoral register. If you are eligible to vote, you can register by contacting your local council election registration office. If you don't know what your local authority is, you can find out by telephoning the Local Government Association (LGA) information line on 020 7664 3131 between 9 a.m. and 5 p.m., Monday to Friday. You will have to tell them your postcode or your full address and they will be able to give you the name of your local authority. You can also get voter registration forms in English, Welsh and some other languages on the internet: **www.electoralcommission.org.uk**.

The electoral register is updated every year in September or October. An electoral registration form is sent to every household and it has to be completed and returned, with the names of everyone who is resident in the household and eligible to vote on 15 October.

In Northern Ireland a different system operates. This is called individual registration and all those entitled to vote must complete their own registration form. Once registered, you can stay on the register provided your personal details do not change. For more information telephone the Electoral Office for Northern Ireland on 028 9044 6688.

By law, each local authority has to make its electoral register available for anyone to look at, although this now has to be supervised. The register is kept at each local electoral registration office (or council office in England and Wales). It is also possible to see the register at some public buildings such as libraries.

Standing for office

Most citizens of the United Kingdom, the Irish Republic or the Commonwealth aged 18 or over can stand for public office. There are some exceptions and these include members of the armed forces, civil servants and people found guilty of certain criminal offences. Members of the House of Lords may not stand for election to the House of Commons but are eligible for all other public offices.

To become a local councillor, a candidate must have a local connection with the area through work, being on the electoral register, or through renting or owning land or property.

Contacting elected members

All elected members have a duty to serve and represent their constituents. You can get contact details for all your representatives and their parties from your local library. Assembly members, MSPs, MPs and MEPs are also listed in the phone book and Yellow Pages. You can contact MPs by letter or phone at their constituency office or their office in the House of Commons: The House of Commons, Westminster, London SW1A 0AA, or telephone: 020 7729 3000. Many Assembly Members, MSPs, MPs and MEPs hold regular local 'surgeries'. These are often advertised in the local paper and constituents can go and talk about issues in person. You can find out the name of your local MP and get in touch with them by fax through the website: **www.writetothem.com**. This service is free.

How to visit Parliament and the Devolved Administrations

- The public can listen to debates in the Palace of Westminster from public galleries in both the House of Commons and the House of Lords. You can either write to your local MP in advance to ask for tickets or you can queue on the day at the public entrance. Entrance is free. Sometimes there are long queues for the House of Commons and you may have to wait for at least one or two hours. It is usually easier to get into the House of Lords. You can find further information on the UK Parliament website: **www.parliament.uk**.

- In Northern Ireland, elected members, known as MLAs, meet in the Northern Ireland Assembly at Stormont, in Belfast. The Northern Ireland Assembly is presently suspended. There are two ways to arrange a visit to Stormont. You can either contact the Education Service (details on the Northern Ireland Assembly website: **www.niassembly.gov.uk**) or contact an MLA

- In Scotland, the elected members, called MSPs, meet in the Scottish Parliament at Holyrood in Edinburgh (for more information see: **www.scottish.parliament.uk**). You can get information, book tickets or arrange tours through the visitor services. You can write to them at The Scottish Parliament, Edinburgh, EH99 1SP, or telephone 0131 348 5200, or email sp.bookings@scottish.parliament.uk

- In Wales, the elected members, known as AMs, meet in the Welsh Assembly in the Senedd in Cardiff Bay (for more information see: **www.wales.gov.uk**). You can book guided tours or seats in the public galleries for the Welsh Assembly. To make a booking, telephone the Assembly booking line on 029 2089 8477 or email: assembly.booking@wales.gsi.gov.uk.

Check that you understand:

- The role of the monarchy
- How Parliament works, and the difference between the House of Commons and the House of Lords
- How often general elections are held
- Where the official residence of the Prime Minister is
- The role of the Cabinet and who is in it
- The nature of the UK constitution
- The job of the Opposition, the Leader of the Opposition and the Shadow Cabinet
- The difference between the 'first past the post' and proportional representation
- The form of electoral systems in the devolved administrations in Northern Ireland, Scotland and Wales
- The rights and duties of British citizens, including naturalised citizens
- How the judiciary, police and local authorities work
- What non-departmental public bodies are

Test yourself

Now that you have studied this section, go to page 139 to find the practice questions that refer to this material and check that you have understood all the information.

If you have any problems with answering the questions about this section you should read through it again, paying particular attention to the areas pointed out in the 'Check that you understand' box.

The UK in Europe and the world

The Commonwealth

The Commonwealth is an association of countries, most of which were once part of the British Empire, though a few countries that were not in the Empire have joined it.

Commonwealth Members

Antigua and Barbuda
Australia
The Bahamas
Bangladesh
Barbados
Belize
Botswana
Brunei Darussalam
Cameroon
Canada
Cyprus
Dominica
Fiji Islands
The Gambia
Ghana
Grenada
Guyana
India
Jamaica
Kenya
Kiribati
Lesotho
Malawi
Malaysia
Maldives
Malta
Mauritius

Mozambique
Namibia
Nauru*
New Zealand
Nigeria
Pakistan
Papua New Guinea
St Kitts and Nevis
St Lucia
St Vincent and the Grenadines
Samoa
Seychelles
Sierra Leone
Singapore
Solomon Islands
South Africa
Sri Lanka
Swaziland
Tonga
Trinidad and Tobago
Tuvalu
Uganda
United Kingdom
United Republic of Tanzania
Vanuatu
Zambia
*Nauru is a Special Member

The Queen is the head of the Commonwealth, which currently has 53 member states. Membership is voluntary and the Commonwealth has no power over its members although it can suspend membership. The Commonwealth aims to promote democracy, good government and to eradicate poverty.

More information

A very important event in the Commonwealth calendar is the Commonwealth Games, which are held every four years in a different country of the Commonwealth. Manchester held a very successful event in 2002 and the Games will take place in Delhi in 2010.

The aim is to develop sport for the benefit of the people, the nations and the territories of the Commonwealth and thereby strengthen the Commonwealth.

The European Union (EU)

The European Union (EU), originally called the European Economic Community (EEC), was set up by six Western European countries who signed the Treaty of Rome on 25 March 1957. One of the main reasons for doing this was the belief that co-operation between states would reduce the likelihood of another war in Europe. Originally the UK decided not to join this group and only became part of the European Union in 1973. In 2004 ten new member countries joined the EU, with a further two in 2006 making a total of 27 member countries.

European Union Members in 2007

The EEC was formed in 1957 and had only six members. Now, in 2007, there are 27 member states of the EU:

Austria	Italy
Belgium	Latvia
Bulgaria	Lithuania
Cyprus	Luxembourg
Czech republic	Malta
Estonia	Netherlands
Denmark	Poland
Finland	Portugal
France	Romania
Germany	Slovakia
Greece	Slovenia
Hungary	Spain
Ireland	Sweden

And, of course, the United Kingdom

One of the main aims of the EU today is for member states to function as a single market. Most of the countries of the EU have a shared currency, the euro, but the UK has decided to retain its own currency unless the British people choose to accept the euro in a referendum. Citizens of an EU member state have the right to travel to and work in any EU country if they have a valid passport or identity card. This right can be restricted on the grounds of public health, public order and public security. The right to work is also sometimes restricted for citizens of countries that have joined the EU recently.

The Council of the European Union (usually called the Council of Ministers) is effectively the governing body off the EU. It is made up of government ministers from each country in the EU and, together with the European Parliament, is the legislative body of the EU. The Council of Ministers passes EU law on the recommendations of the European Commission and the European Parliament and takes the most important decisions about how the EU is run. The European Commission is based in Brussels, the capital city of Belgium. It is the civil service of the EU and drafts proposals for new EU policies and laws and administers its funding programmes.

The European Parliament meets in Strasbourg, in north-eastern France, and in Brussels. Each country elects members, called Members of the European Parliament (MEPs), every five years. The European Parliament examines decisions made by the European Council and the European Commission, and it has the power to refuse agreement to European laws proposed by the Commission and to check on the spending of EU funds.

European Union law is legally binding in the UK and all the other member states. European laws, called directives, regulations or framework decisions, have made a lot of difference to people's rights in the UK, particularly at work. For example, there are EU directives about the procedures for making workers redundant, and regulations that limit the number of hours people can be made to work.

The Council of Europe

The Council of Europe was created in 1949 and the UK was one of the founder members. Most of the countries of Europe are members. It has no power to make laws but draws up conventions and charters which focus on human rights, democracy, education, the environment, health and culture. The most important of these is the European Convention on Human Rights; all member states are bound by this convention and a member state which persistently refuses to obey the convention may be expelled from the Council of Europe.

The United Nations (UN)

The UK is a member of the United Nations (UN), an international organisation to which over 190 countries now belong. The UN was set up after the Second World War and aims to prevent war and promote international peace and security. There are 15 members on the UN Security Council, which recommends action by the UN when there are international crises and threats to peace. The UK is one of the permanent members.

Three very important agreements produced by the UN are the Universal Declaration of Human Rights, the Convention on the Elimination of All Forms of Discrimination against Women, and the UN Convention on the Rights of the Child. Although none of these has the force of law, they are widely used in political debate and legal cases to reinforce the law and to assess the behaviour of countries.

Check that you understand:

- The differences between the Council of Europe, the European Union, the European Commission and the European Parliament
- The UK is a member of the Council of Europe and the European Union
- The EU aims to become a single market and it is administered by a Council of Ministers of governments of member states
- Subject to some restrictions, EU citizens may travel to and work in any EU country
- The roles of the UN and the Commonwealth

Test yourself

Now that you have studied this section, go to page 149 to find the practice questions that refer to this material and check that you have understood all the information.

If you have any problems with answering the questions about this section you should read through it again, paying particular attention to the areas pointed out in the 'Check that you understand' box.

Summary

This section of *Life in the UK* concentrates on the system of government used in the UK and contains a lot of complicated information involving the roles played in the UK by the monarchy, Europe, devolved administration and the UK constitution.

It is essential that you are clear about the various European organisations and the part they play in the government of the UK – it may help if you summarise this section of information in your own words so that you are sure that you have grasped it. You may also find the glossary at the end of this book useful as many of the institutions discussed in this section are defined there.

06

everyday needs (from *Life in the UK*)

In this chapter you will:
- find out about buying or renting a home in the UK
- learn how healthcare is delivered
- understand how the UK's education system works.

Overview

The material in this fourth chapter from *Life in the* UK concentrates on more everyday matters than the previous ones. There is information in this chapter on things that will affect your day-to-day life such as health, education, buying or renting a home and spending your leisure time. It is important that you understand that there are differences in many of the ways in which services such as education are provided in the different parts of the UK. Northern Ireland, Wales, England and Scotland all have slightly different methods in many important areas, so you should note these as you go through the material.

Now on to the official information that comes from Chapter 5: Everyday Needs, in the Home Office publication *Life in the United Kingdom – A Journey to Citizenship*.

****

In this chapter there is information about:

- Housing
- Services in and for the home
- Money and credit
- Health
- Pregnancy and care of young children
- Education
- Leisure
- Travel and transport
- Identity documents

Housing

Buying a home

Two-thirds of people in the UK own their own home. Most other people rent houses, flats or rooms.

Mortgages

People who buy their own homes usually pay for it with a mortgage, a special loan from a bank or building society. This loan is paid back, with interest, over a long period of time, usually 25 years. You can get information about mortgages from a bank or building society. Some banks can also give you information about Islamic (Sharia) mortgages.

75

More information

Interest is the charge that banks and building societies make for lending you money. A mortgage usually has a low rate of interest compared with other types of loan. It is important to check the rate of interest that you will be paying so that you are not paying too much.

If you are having problems paying your mortgage repayments, you can get help and advice. It is important to speak to your bank or building society as soon as you can.

Estate agents

If you wish to buy a home, usually the first place to start is an estate agent. In Scotland the process is different and you should go first to a solicitor. Estate agents represent the person selling their house or flat. They arrange for buyers to visit homes that are for sale. There are estate agents in all towns and cities and they usually have websites where they advertise the homes for sale. You can also find details about homes for sale on the internet and in national and local newspapers.

Making an offer

In the UK, except in Scotland, when you find a home you wish to buy you have to make an offer to the seller. You usually do this through an estate agent or solicitor. Many people offer a lower price than the seller is asking. Your first offer must be 'subject to contract' so that you can withdraw if there are reasons why you cannot complete the purchase. In Scotland the seller sets a price and buyers make offers over that amount. The agreement becomes legally binding earlier than it does elsewhere in the UK.

Solicitor and surveyor

It is important that a solicitor helps you through the process of buying a house or flat. When you make an offer on a property, the solicitor will carry out a number of legal checks on the property, the seller and the local area. The solicitor will provide the legal agreements necessary for you to buy the property. The bank or building society that is providing you with your mortgage will also carry out checks on the house or flat you wish to buy. These are done by a surveyor. The buyer does not usually see the result of this survey, so the buyer often asks a second surveyor to check the house as well. In Scotland the survey is carried out before an offer is made, to help people decide how much they want to bid for the property.

Rented accommodation

It is possible to rent accommodation from the local authority (the council), from a housing association or from private property owners called landlords.

The local authority

Most local authorities (or councils) provide housing. This is often called 'council housing'. In Northern Ireland social housing is provided by the Northern Ireland Housing Executive (**www.nihe.gov.uk**). In Scotland you can find information on social housing at: **www.sfha.co.uk**. Everyone is entitled to apply for council accommodation. To apply you must put your name on a council register or list. This is available from the housing department at the local authority. You are then assessed according to your needs. This is done through a system of points. You get more points if you have priority needs, for example if you are homeless and have children or chronic ill health.

It is important to note that in many areas of the UK there is a shortage of council accommodation, and that some people have to wait a very long time for a house or flat.

Housing associations

Housing associations are independent not-for-profit organisations which provide housing for rent. In some areas they have taken over the administration of local authority housing. They also run schemes called shared ownership, which help people to buy part of a house or flat if they cannot afford to buy all of it at once. There are usually waiting lists for homes owned by housing associations.

Privately rented accommodation

Many people rent houses or flats privately, from landlords. Information about private accommodation can be found in local newspapers, notice boards, estate agents and letting agents.

Tenancy agreement

When you rent a house or flat privately you sign a tenancy agreement, or lease. This explains the conditions or 'rules' you must follow while renting the property. This agreement must be checked very carefully to avoid problems later. The agreement also contains a list of any furniture or fittings in the property. This is called an inventory. Before you sign the agreement, check the details and keep it safe during your tenancy.

Deposit and rent

You will probably be asked to give the landlord a deposit at the beginning of your tenancy. This is to cover the cost of any damage. It is usually equal to one month's rent. The landlord must return this money to you at the end of your tenancy, unless you have caused damage to the property.

Your rent is fixed with your landlord at the beginning of the tenancy. The landlord cannot raise the rent without your agreement.

If you have a low income or are unemployed you may be able to claim Housing Benefit to help you pay your rent.

Renewing and ending a tenancy

Your tenancy agreement will be for a fixed period of time, often six months. After this time the tenancy can be ended or, if both tenant and landlord agree, renewed. If you end the tenancy before the fixed time, you usually have to pay the rent for the agreed full period of the tenancy.

A landlord cannot force a tenant to leave. If a landlord wishes a tenant to leave they must follow the correct procedures. These vary according to the type of tenancy. It is a criminal offence to use threats or violence against a tenant or to force them to leave without an order from a court.

Discrimination

It is unlawful for a landlord to discriminate against someone looking for accommodation because of their sex, race, nationality, or ethnic group, or because they are disabled, unless the landlord or a close relative of the landlord is sharing the accommodation.

Homelessness

If you are homeless you should go for help to the local authority (or, in Northern Ireland, the Housing Executive). They have a legal duty to offer help and advice, but will not offer you a place to live unless you have priority need (see above) and have a connection with the area, such as work or family. You must also show that you have not made yourself intentionally homeless.

Help

If you are homeless or have problems with your landlord, help can be found from the following:

- The housing department of the local authority will give advice on homelessness and on Housing Benefit as well as deal with problems you may have in council-owned property
- The Citizens Advice Bureau will give advice on all types of housing problems. There may also be a housing advice centre in your neighbourhood
- Shelter is a housing charity which runs a 24-hour helpline on 0808 800 4444, or visit **www.shelternet.org.uk**.
- Help with the cost of moving and setting up home may be available from the Social Fund. This is run by the Department for Work and Pensions (DWP). It provides grants and loans such as the Community Care Grant for people setting up home after being homeless or after they have been in prison or other institutions. Other loans are available for people who have had an emergency such as flooding. Information about these is available at the Citizens Advice Bureau or Jobcentre Plus.

Services in and for the home

Water

Water is supplied to all homes in the UK. The charge for this is called the water rates. When you move in to a new home (bought or rented), you should receive a letter telling you the name of the company responsible for supplying your water. The water rates may be paid in one payment (a lump sum) or in instalments, usually monthly. If you receive Housing Benefit, you should check to see if this covers the water rates. The cost of the water usually depends on the size of your property, but some homes have a water meter which tells you exactly how much water you have used. In Northern Ireland water is currently (2006) included in the domestic rates, although this may change in future.

Electricity and gas

All properties in the UK have electricity supplied at 240 volts. Most homes also have gas. When you move into a new home or leave an old one, you should make a note of the electricity and gas meter readings. If you have an urgent problem with your gas, electricity or water supply, you can ring a 24-hour helpline. This can be found on your bill, in the Yellow Pages or in the phone book.

Gas and electricity suppliers

It is possible to choose between different gas and electricity suppliers. These have different prices and different terms and conditions. Get advice before you sign a contract with a new supplier. To find out which company supplies your gas, telephone Transco on 0870 608 1524

To find out which company supplies your electricity, telephone Energywatch on 0845 906 0708 or visit: **www.energywatch. org.uk**. Energywatch can also give you advice on changing your supplier of electricity or gas.

Telephone

Most homes already have a telephone line (called a land line). If you need a new line, telephone BT on 150 442, or contact a cable company. Many companies offer landline, mobile telephone and broadband internet services. You can get advice about prices or about changing your company from Ofcom at: **www.ofcom.org.uk**. You can call from public payphones using cash, pre-paid phonecards or credit or debit cards. Calls made from hotels and hostels are usually more expensive. Dial 999 or 112 for emergency calls for police, fire or ambulance service.

These calls are free. Do not use these numbers if it is not a real emergency; you can always find the local numbers for these services in the phone book.

Bills

Information on how to pay for water, gas, electricity and the telephone is found on the back of each bill. If you have a bank account you can pay your bills by standing order or direct debit. Most companies operate a budget scheme which allows you to pay a fixed sum every month. If you do not pay a bill, the service can be cut off. To get a service reconnected, you have to pay another charge.

Refuse collection

Refuse is also called waste, or rubbish. The local authority collects the waste regularly, usually on the same day of each week. Waste must be put outside in a particular place to get collected. In some parts of the country the waste is put into plastic bags, in others it is put into bins with wheels. In many places you must recycle your rubbish, separating paper, glass, metal or plastic from the other rubbish. Large objects which you want to throw away, such as a bed, wardrobe or a fridge, need to be collected separately. Contact the local authority to arrange this. If you have a business, such as a factory or a shop, you must make special arrangements with the local authority for your waste to be collected. It is a criminal offence to dump rubbish anywhere.

Why recycle?

Each UK household produces over 1 tonne of rubbish annually, amounting to about 31 million tonnes for the UK each year. This is a huge volume of waste and in order to prevent all of it going into landfill sites, we should recycle as much as possible.

Council Tax

Local government services such as education, police, roads, refuse collections and libraries, are paid for partly by grants from the government and partly by Council Tax. In Northern Ireland there is a system of domestic rates instead of the Council

Tax. The amount of the Council Tax you pay depends on the size and value of your house or flat (dwelling). You must register to pay Council Tax when you move into a new property, either as the owner or the tenant. You can pay the tax in one payment, in two instalments, or in ten instalments (from April to January).

If only one person lives in the flat or house, you get a 25% reduction on your Council Tax. (This does not apply in Northern Ireland). You may also get a reduction if someone in the property has a disability. People on a low income or who receive benefits such as Income Support or Jobseeker's Allowance can get Council Tax Benefit. You can get advice on this from the local authority or the Citizens Advice Bureau.

Buildings and household insurance

If you buy a home with a mortgage, you must insure the building against fire, theft and accidental damage. The landlord should arrange insurance for rented buildings. It is also wise to insure your possessions against theft or damage. There are many companies that provide insurance.

Neighbours

If you live in rented accommodation, you will have a tenancy agreement. This explains all the conditions of your tenancy. It will probably include information on what to do if you have problems with your housing. Occasionally, there may be problems with your neighbours. If you do have problems with your neighbours, they can usually be solved by speaking to them first. If you cannot solve the problem, speak to your landlord, local authority or housing association. Keep a record of the problems in case you have to show exactly what the problems are and when they started. Neighbours who cause a very serious nuisance may be taken to court and can be evicted from their home.

There are several mediation organisations which help neighbours to solve their disputes without having to go to court. Mediators talk to both sides and try to find a solution acceptable to both. You can get details of mediation from the local authority, Citizens Advice, and Mediation UK on 0117 904 6661.

Check that you understand:

- The process for buying and renting accommodation
- Where to get advice about accommodation and moving
- The role of an estate agent
- Housing priorities for local authorities
- Where to get help if you are homeless
- How you can pay for the water you use at home
- Recycling your waste
- What Council Tax pays for
- What to do if you have problems with your neighbours

Test yourself

Now that you have studied this section, go to page 151 to find the practice questions that refer to this material and check that you have understood all the information.

If you have any problems with answering the questions about this section you should read through it again, paying particular attention to the areas pointed out in the 'Check that you understand' box.

Money and credit

Bank notes in the UK come in denominations (values) of £5, £10, £20 and £50. Northern Ireland and Scotland have their own bank notes which are valid everywhere in the UK, though sometimes people may not realise this and may not wish to accept them.

The euro

In January 2002 twelve European Union (EU) states adopted the euro as their common currency. The UK government decided not to adopt the euro at that time, and has said it will only do so if the British people vote for the euro in a referendum. The euro does circulate to some extent in Northern Ireland, particularly in the towns near the border with Ireland.

Foreign currency

You can get or change foreign currency at banks, building societies, large post offices and exchange shops or bureaux de change. You might have to order some currencies in advance. The exchange rates vary and you should check for the best deal.

Banks and building societies

Most adults in the UK have a bank or building society account. Many large national banks or building societies have branches in towns and cities throughout the UK. It is worth checking the different types of account each one offers. Many employers pay salaries directly into a bank or building society account. There are many banks and building societies to choose from. To open an account, you need to show documents to prove your identity, such as a passport, immigration document or driving licence. You also need to show something with your address on it like a tenancy agreement or household bill. It is also possible to open bank accounts in some supermarkets or on the internet.

Cash and debit cards

Cash cards allow you to use cash machines to withdraw money from your account. For this you need a Personal Identification Number (PIN) which you must keep secret. A debit card allows you to pay for things without using cash. You must have enough money in your account to cover what you buy. If you lose your cash card or debit card you must inform the bank immediately.

Credit and store cards

Credit cards can be used to buy things in shops, on the telephone and over the internet. A store card is like a credit card but used only in a specific shop. Credit and store cards do not draw money from your bank account, but you will be sent a bill every month. If you do not pay the total amount on the bill, you are charged interest. Although credit and store cards are useful, the interest is usually very high and many people fall into debt this way. If you lose your credit or store cards you must inform the company immediately.

Credit and loans

People in the UK often borrow money from banks and other organisations to pay for things like household goods, cars and holidays. This is more common in the UK than in many other countries. You must be very sure of the terms and conditions when you decide to take out a loan. You can get advice on loans from the Citizens Advice Bureau if you are uncertain.

Being refused credit

Banks and other organisations use different information about you to make a decision about a loan, such as your occupation, address, salary and previous credit record. If you apply for a loan you might be refused. If this happens, you have the right to ask the reason why.

Credit unions

Credit unions are financial co-operatives owned and controlled by their members. The members pool their savings and then make loans from this pool. Interest rates in credit unions are usually lower than banks and building societies. There are credit unions in many cities and towns. To find the nearest credit union contact the Association of British Credit Unions (ABCUL) on: **www.abcul.coop**.

More information

Consumer debt (the money owed by private individuals) has risen sharply over recent years and is now over £1 trillion (£1,000 billion). Approximately 80% of this is owed as mortgages on homes.

According to the National Consumer Council, over six million families are struggling to keep up with credit commitments and the scale of this problem is causing a lot of concern.

Insurance

As well as insuring their property and possessions (see above), many people insure their credit cards and mobile phones. They also buy insurance when they travel abroad in case they lose their luggage or need medical treatment. Insurance is compulsory if you have a car or motorcycle. You can usually arrange insurance directly with an insurance company, or you can use a broker who will help you get the best deal.

Social security

The UK has a system of social security which pays welfare benefits to people who do not have enough money to live on. Benefits are usually available for the sick and disabled, older people, the unemployed and those on low incomes. People who do not have legal rights of residence (or 'settlement') in the UK cannot usually receive benefits. Arrangements for paying and receiving benefits are complex because they have to cover people in many different situations. Guides to benefits are available from Jobcentre Plus offices, local libraries, post offices and the Citizens Advice Bureau.

Check that you understand:

- What you need to open a bank or building society account
- What debit, credit and store cards are
- What a credit union is
- What insurance is
- How to get help with benefits and problems with debt

Test yourself

Now that you have studied this section, go to page 153 to find the practice questions that refer to this material and check that you have understood all the information.

If you have any problems with answering the questions about this section you should read through it again, paying particular attention to the areas pointed out in the 'Check that you understand' box.

Health

Healthcare in the UK is organised under the National Health Service (NHS). The NHS began in 1948, and is one of the largest organisations in Europe. It provides all residents with free healthcare and treatment.

Finding a doctor

Family doctors are called General Practitioners (GPs) and they work in surgeries. GPs often work together in a group practice. This is sometimes called a Primary Health Care Centre.

Your GP is responsible for organising the health treatment you receive. Treatment can be for physical and mental illnesses. If you need to see a specialist, you must go to your GP first. Your GP will then refer you to a specialist in a hospital. Your GP can also refer you for specialist treatment if you have special needs.

You can get a list of local GPs from libraries, post offices, the tourist information office, the Citizens Advice Bureau, the local Health Authority and from the following websites:

www.nhs.uk/ for health practitioners in England;

www.wales.nhs.uk/directory.cfm for health practitioners in Wales;

www.n-i.nhs.uk for health practitioners in Northern Ireland;

www.show.scot.nhs.uk/findnearest/healthservices in Scotland.

You can also ask neighbours and friends for the name of their local doctor.

You can attend a hospital without a GP's letter only in the case of an emergency. If you have an emergency you should go to the Accident and Emergency (A & E) department of the nearest hospital.

Registering with a GP

You should look for a GP as soon as you move to a new area. You should not wait until you are ill. The health centre, or surgery, will tell you what you need to do to register. Usually you must have a medical card. If you do not have one, the GPs receptionist should give you a form to send to the local health authority. They will then send you a medical card.

Before you register you should check the surgery can offer what you need. For example, you might need a woman GP, or maternity services. Sometimes GPs have many patients and are unable to accept new ones. If you cannot find a GP, you can ask your local health authority to help you find one.

Using your doctor

All patients registering with a GP are entitled to a free health check. Appointments to see the GP can be made by phone or in person. Sometimes you might have to wait several days before you can see a doctor. If you need immediate medical attention ask for an urgent appointment. You should go to the GPs surgery a few minutes before the appointment. If you cannot attend or do not need the appointment any more, you must let the surgery know. The GP needs patients to answer all questions as fully as possible in order to find out what is wrong. Everything you tell the GP is completely confidential and cannot be passed on to anyone else without your permission. If you do not understand something, ask for clarification. If you have difficulties with English, bring someone who can help you, or ask the receptionist for an interpreter. This must be done when you make the appointment. If you have asked for an interpreter, it is important that you keep your appointment because this service is expensive.

In exceptional circumstances, GPs can visit patients at home but they always give priority to people who are unable to travel. If you call the GP outside normal working hours, you will have to answer several questions about your situation. This is to assess how serious your case is. You will then be told if a doctor can come to your home. You might be advised to go to the nearest A & E department.

Charges

Treatment from the GP is free but you have to pay a charge for your medicines and for certain services, such as vaccinations for travel abroad. If the GP decides you need to take medicines you will be given a prescription. You must take this to a pharmacy (chemist).

Prescriptions

Prescriptions are free for anyone who is

- under 16 years of age (under 25 in Wales)
- under 19 and in full-time education
- aged 60 or over
- pregnant or with a baby under 12 months old
- suffering from a specified medical condition
- receiving Income Support, Jobseekers' Allowance, Working Families or Disabilities Tax Credit

Feeling unwell

If you or your child feels unwell you have the following options:

For information and advice

- ask your local pharmacist (chemist). The pharmacy can give advice on medicines and some illnesses and conditions that are not serious
- speak to a nurse by phoning NHS Direct on 0845 46 47
- use the NHS Direct website, NHS Direct Online: **www.nhsdirect.nhs.uk**.

To see a doctor or nurse

- make an appointment to see your GP or a nurse working in the surgery
- visit an NHS walk-in centre.

For urgent medical treatment

- contact your GP
- go to your nearest hospital with an Accident and Emergency department
- call 999 for an ambulance. Calls are free. ONLY use this service for a real emergency.

NHS Direct is a 24-hour telephone service which provides information on particular health conditions. Telephone: 0845 46 47. You may ask for an interpreter for advice in your own language. In Scotland, NHS24 at: **www.nhs24.com** telephone 08454 24 24 24.

NHS Direct Online is a website providing information about health services and several medical conditions and treatments: **www.nhsdirect.nhs.uk**

NHS walk-in centres provide treatment for minor injuries and illnesses seven days a week. You do not need an appointment. For details of your nearest centre call NHS Direct or visit the NHS website at: **www.nhs.uk** (for Northern Ireland **www.n-i.nhs.uk**) and click on 'local NHS services'.

Going into hospital

If you need minor tests at a hospital, you will probably attend the Outpatients department. If your treatment takes several hours, you will go into hospital as a day patient. If you need to stay overnight, you will go into hospital as an in-patient.

You should take personal belongings with you, such as a towel, night clothes, things for washing, and a dressing gown. You will receive all your meals while you are an in-patient. If you need advice about going into hospital, contact Customer Services or the Patient Advice and Liaison Service (PALS) at the hospital where you will receive treatment.

Dentists

You can get the name of a dentist by asking at the local library, at the Citizens Advice Bureau and through NHS Direct. Most people have to pay for dental treatment. Some dentists work for the NHS and some are private. NHS dentists charge less than private dentists, but some dentists have two sets of charges, both NHS and private. A dentist should explain your treatment and the charges before the treatment begins.

Free dental treatment is available to

- people under 18 (in Wales people under 25 and over 60)
- pregnant women and women with babies under 12 months old
- people on income support, Jobseekers' Allowance or Pension Credit Guarantee.

Opticians

Most people have to pay for sight tests and glasses, except children, people over 60, people with certain eye conditions and people receiving certain benefits. In Scotland, eye tests are free.

Pregnancy and care of young children

If you are pregnant you will receive regular antenatal care. This is available from your local hospital, local health centre or from special antenatal clinics. You will receive support from a GP and from a midwife. Midwives work in hospitals or health centres. Some GPs do not provide maternity services so you may wish to look for another GP during your pregnancy. In the UK women usually have their babies in hospital, especially if it is their first baby. It is common for the father to attend the birth but only if the mother wants him to be there.

A short time after you have your child, you will begin regular contact with a health visitor. She or he is a qualified nurse and can advise you about caring for your baby. The first visits will be in your home, but after that you might meet the health visitor at a clinic. You can ask advice from your health visitor until your child is five years old. In most towns and cities there are mother and toddler groups or playgroups for small children. These often take place at local churches and community centres. You might be able to send your child to a nursery school (see Going to School later in this chapter).

Information on pregnancy

You can get information on maternity and antenatal services in your area from your local health authority, a health visitor or your GP. The number of your health authority will be in the phone book.

The Family Planning Association (FPA) gives advice on contraception and sexual health. The FPA's helpline is 0845 310 1334, or: **www.fpa.org.uk**.

The National Childbirth Trust gives information and support in pregnancy, childbirth and early parenthood: **www.nctpregnancy andbabycare.com**.

Registering a birth

You must register your baby with the Registrar of Births, Marriages and Deaths (Register Office) within six weeks of the birth. The address of your local Register Office is in the phone book. If the parents are married, either the mother or father can register the birth. If they are not married, only the mother can register the birth. If the parents are not married but want both names on the child's birth certificate, both mother and father must be present when they register the baby.

Check that you understand:
- How to find and register with a GP
- What to do if you feel unwell
- How to find other services such as dentists and opticians
- When it is possible to attend A & E without a doctor's letter
- Who can get free prescriptions
- When you should phone 999 or 112
- What NHS Direct can do
- Who can give health advice and treatment when you are pregnant and after you have a baby
- How to register a birth

Education

Going to school

Education in the UK is free and compulsory for all children between the ages of 5 and 16 (4 to 16 in Northern Ireland). The education system varies in England, Scotland, Wales and Northern Ireland.

The child's parent or guardian is responsible for making sure their child goes to school, arrives on time and attends for the whole school year. If they do not do this, the parent or guardian may be prosecuted.

Some areas of the country offer free nursery education for children over the age of 3. In most parts of the UK, compulsory education is divided into two stages, primary and secondary. In some places there is a middle-school system. In England and Wales the primary stage lasts from 5 to 11, in Scotland from 5 to 12 and in Northern Ireland from 4 to 11. The secondary stage lasts until the age of 16. At that age young people can choose to leave school or to continue with their education until they are 17 or 18.

Details of local schools are available from your local education authority office or website. The addresses and phone numbers of local education authorities are in the phone book.

Primary schools

These are usually schools where both boys and girls learn together and are usually close to a child's home. Children tend to be with the same group and teacher all day. Schools encourage parents to help their children with learning, particularly with reading and writing.

Secondary schools

At age 11 (12 in Scotland) children go to secondary school. This might normally be the school nearest their home, but parents in England and Wales are allowed to express a preference for a different school. In some areas, getting a secondary school place in a preferred school can be difficult, and parents often apply to several schools in order to make sure their child gets offered a place. In Northern Ireland many schools select children through a test taken at the age of 11.

If the preferred school has enough places, the child will be offered a place. If there are not enough places, children will be offered places according to the school's admission arrangements. Admission arrangements vary from area to area.

Secondary schools are larger than primary schools. Most are mixed sex, although there are single sex schools in some areas. Your local education authority will give you information on schools in your area. It will also tell you which schools have spaces and give you information about why some children will be given places when only a few are available and why other children might not. It will also tell you how to apply for a secondary school place.

Costs

Education at state schools in the UK is free, but parents have to pay for school uniforms and sports wear. There are sometimes extra charges for music lessons and for school outings. Parents on low incomes can get help with costs, and with the cost of school meals. You can get advice on this from the local education authority or the Citizens Advice Bureau.

Church and other faith schools

Some primary and secondary schools in the UK are linked to the Church of England or the Roman Catholic Church. These are called 'faith schools'. In some areas there are Muslim, Jewish and Sikh schools. In Northern Ireland some schools are called Integrated Schools. These schools aim to bring children of different religions together. Information on faith schools is available from your local education authority.

Independent schools

Independent schools are private schools. They are not run or paid for by the state. Independent secondary schools are also sometimes called public schools. There are about 2,500 independent schools in the UK. About 8% of children go to these schools. At independent schools parents must pay the full cost of their child's education. Some independent schools offer scholarships which pay some or all of the costs of the child's education.

The school curriculum

All state, primary and secondary schools in England, Wales and Northern Ireland follow the National Curriculum. This covers English, maths, science, design and technology, information and communication technology (ICT), history, geography, modern foreign languages, art and design, music, physical education (PE) and citizenship. In Wales, children learn Welsh.

In some primary schools in Wales, all the lessons are taught in Welsh. In Scotland, pupils follow a broad curriculum informed by national guidance. Schools must, by law, provide religious education (RE) to all pupils. Parents are allowed to withdraw their children from these lessons. RE lessons have a Christian basis but children also learn about the other major religions.

Assessment

In England the curriculum is divided into four stages, called Key Stages. After each stage children are tested. They take Key Stage tests (also called SATs) at ages 7, 11 and 14. At 16 they usually take the General Certificates of Secondary Educations (GCSEs) in several subjects, although some schools offer other qualifications. At 18, young people who have stayed at school do AGCEs (advanced GCE levels) often just called A levels.

In Wales, schools follow the Welsh National Curriculum but have abolished national tests for children at age 7 and 11. There are also plans in Wales to stop testing at 14. Teachers in Wales still have to assess and report on their pupils' progress and achievements at 7 and 11.

In Scotland, the curriculum is divided into two phases. The first phase is from 5 to 14. There are six levels in this phase, levels A to F. There are no tests for whole groups during this time.

Teachers test individual children when they are ready. From 14 to 16, young people do Standard Grade. After 16 they can study at Intermediate, Higher or Advanced level. In Scotland there will soon be a single curriculum for all pupils from age 3 to age 18. This is called A Curriculum for Excellence. More information can be found at: **www.acurriculumfor excellencescotland.gov.uk**.

More information

With testing taking place at the ages of 7, 11, 14, 16 and 18, children at schools in England are among the most tested children in the world and there have been calls for the system to be revised, with – as is the system in Wales – more informal assessment taking place in the classroom rather than formal examinations and tests.

Help with English

If your child's main language is not English, the school may arrange for extra language support from an EAL (English Additional Language) specialist teacher.

Careers education

All children get careers advice from the age of 14. Advice is also available from Connexions, a national service for young people: telephone 080 800 13219 or: **www.connexions-direct.com** in England. In Wales, Careers Wales offers advice to children from the age of 11. For further information visit: **www.careerswales.com** or telephone 0800 100 900.

In Scotland, Careers Scotland provides information, services and support to all ages and stages. For further information visit: **www.careers-scotland.org.uk** or telephone 0845 8 502 502.

Parents and schools

Many parents are involved with their child's school. A number of places on a school's governing body are reserved for parents. The governing body decides how the school is run and administered and produces reports on the progress of the school from year to year. In Scotland, parents can be members of school boards or parent councils.

Schools must be open 190 days a year. Term dates are decided by the governing body or by the local education authority. Children must attend the whole school year. Schools expect parents and guardians to inform them if their child is going to be absent from school. All schools ask parents to sign a home-school agreement. This is a list of things that both the school and the parent or guardian agree to do to ensure a good education for the child. All parents receive a report every year on their child's progress. They also have the chance to go to the school to talk to their child's teachers.

Further education and adult education

At 16, young people can leave school or stay on to do A levels (Higher grades in Scotland) in preparation for university. Some young people go to their local further education (FE) college to improve their exam grades or to get new qualifications for a career. Most courses are free up to the age of 19. Young people from families with low incomes can get financial help with their studies when they leave school at 16. This is called the Education Maintenance Allowance (EMA). Information about this is available at your local college or at: **www.dfes.gov.uk**.

Further education colleges also offer courses to adults over the age of 18. These include courses for people wishing to improve their skills in English. These courses are called ESOL (English for Speakers of Other Languages). There are also courses for English speakers who need to improve their literacy and numeracy and for people who need to learn new skills for employment. ESOL courses are also available in community centres and training centres. There is sometimes a waiting list for ESOL course because demand is high. In England and Wales, ESOL, literacy and numeracy courses are called Skills for Life courses. You can get information at your local college or local library or from learndirect on 0800 100 900.

Many people join other adult education classes to learn a new skill or hobby and to meet new people. Classes are very varied and range from sports to learning a musical instrument or a new language. Details are usually available from your local library, college or adult education centre.

University

More young people go to university now than in the past. Many go after A levels (or Higher grades in Scotland) at age 18 but it is also possible to go to university later in life. At present, most students in England, Wales and Northern Ireland have to pay towards the cost of their tuition fees and to pay for their living expenses. In Scotland there are no tuition fees but after students finish university they pay back some of the cost of their education in a payment called an endowment. At present, universities can charge up to £3,000 per year for their tuition fees, but students do not have to pay anything towards their fees before or during their studies. The government pays their tuition fees and then charges for them when a student starts working after university. Some families on low incomes receive help with their children's tuition fees. This is called a grant. The universities also give help, in the form of bursaries. Most students get a low-interest student loan from a bank. This pays for their living costs while they are at university. When a student finishes university and starts working, he or she must pay back the loan.

Check that you understand:

- The different stages of a child's education
- That there are differences in the education systems in England, Scotland, Wales and Northern Ireland
- That there are different kinds of school, and that some of them charge fees
- What the National Curriculum is
- What the governing body of a school does
- Options for young people at the age of 16
- Courses available at FE colleges
- Where you can get English classes or other education for adults, including university

Test yourself

Now that you have studied this section, go to page 155 to find the practice questions that refer to this material and check that you have understood all the information.

If you have any problems with answering the questions about this section you should read through it again, paying particular attention to the areas pointed out in the 'Check that you understand' box.

Leisure

Information

Information about theatre, cinema, music and exhibitions is found in local newspapers, local libraries and tourist information offices. Many museums and art galleries are free.

> **More information**
>
> Many of the services offered in public libraries are free. You can visit a library to get information about courses, local events and lots of other subjects, use a computer or a photocopier or, if you become a member, to borrow books, CDs and DVDs.

Film, video and DVD

Films in the UK have a system to show if they are suitable for children. This is called the classification system. If a child is below the age of the classification, they should not watch the film at a cinema or on DVD. All films receive a classification, as follows:

U (Universal): suitable for anyone aged 4 years and over

PG (parental guidance): suitable for everyone but some parts of the film might be unsuitable for children. Their parents should decide.

12 or 12a: children under 12 are not allowed to see or rent the film unless they are with an adult.

15: children under 15 are not allowed to see or rent the film.

18: no one under 18 is allowed to see or rent the film.

R18: no one under 18 is allowed to see the film, which is only available in specially licensed cinemas.

Television and radio

Anyone in the UK with a television (TV), DVD or video recorder, computer or any device which is used for watching or recording TV programmes must be covered by a valid television licence. One licence covers all of the equipment at one address, but people who rent different rooms in a shared house must each buy a separate licence.

A colour TV licence currently costs £131.50 (2006) and lasts for 12 months. People aged 75 or over can apply for a free TV licence. Blind people can claim a 50% discount on their TV licence. You risk prosecution and a fine if you watch TV but are not covered by a TV licence. There are many ways to buy a TV licence including from local Pay Point outlets or on-line at: **www.tvlicensing.co.uk**. It is also possible to pay for the licence in instalments. For more information telephone 0870 576 3763 or write to TV Licensing, Bristol BS98 1TL

Sports, clubs and societies

Information about local clubs and societies can usually be found at local libraries or through your local authority. For information about sports you should ask in the local leisure centre. Libraries and leisure centres often organise activities for children during the school holidays.

Places of interest

The UK has a large network of public footpaths in the countryside. Many parts of the countryside and places of interest are kept open by the National Trust. This is a charity that works to preserve important buildings and countryside in the UK. Information about National Trust buildings and areas open to the public is available on: **www.nationaltrust.org.uk**.

Pubs and night clubs

Public houses, or pubs, are an important part of social life in the UK. To drink alcohol in a pub you must be 18 or over. People under 18 are not allowed to buy alcohol in a supermarket or in an off-licence either. The landlord of the pub may allow people of 14 to come into the pub but they are not allowed to drink. At 16, people can drink wine or beer with a meal in a hotel or restaurant.

Pubs are usually open during the day and until 11 p.m. If a pub wants to stay open later, it must apply for a special licence. Night clubs open and close later than pubs.

Betting and gambling

People under 18 are not allowed into betting shops or gambling clubs. There is a National Lottery for which draws, with large prizes, are made every week. You can enter by buying a ticket or a scratch card. People under 16 are not allowed to buy a lottery ticket or a scratch card.

Pets

Many people in the UK have pets such as cats and dogs. It is against the law to treat a pet cruelly or to neglect it. All dogs in public places must wear a collar showing the name and address of the owner. The owner is responsible for keeping the dog under control and for cleaning up after the animal in a public place. Vaccinations and medical treatment for animals are available from veterinary surgeons (vets). If you cannot afford to pay a vet, you can go to a charity called the PDSA (People's Dispensary for Sick Animals). To find your nearest branch, visit: **www.pdsa.org.uk**.

Travel and transport

Trains, buses and coaches

For information about trains telephone the National Rail Enquiry Service: 08457 48 49 50, or visit: **www.nationalrail.co.uk**. For trains in Northern Ireland, phone Translink on 028 90 66 66 30 or visit: **www.translink.co.uk**. For information about local bus times phone 0870 608 250. For information on coaches, telephone National Express on 08705 80 80 80, or visit: **www.nationalexpress.com**. For coaches in Scotland, telephone Scottish Citylink on 08705 50 50 50, or visit: **www.citylink.co.uk**. For Northern Ireland, visit: **www.translink.co.uk**.

Usually, tickets for trains and underground systems such as the London Underground must be bought before you get on the train. The fare varies according to the day and time you wish to travel. Travelling in the rush hour is always more expensive. Discount tickets are available for families, people aged 60 and over, disabled people, students and people under 26. Ask at your local train station for details. Failure to buy a ticket may result in a penalty.

Taxis

To operate legally, all taxis and minicabs must be licensed and display a license plate. Taxis and cabs with no licence are not insured for fare-paying passengers and are not always safe. Women should not use unlicensed minicabs.

Driving

You must be at least 17 to drive a car or motorcycle, 18 to drive a medium-sized lorry, and 21 to drive a large lorry or a bus. To drive a lorry, minibus or bus with more than eight passenger seats, you must have a special licence.

The driving licence

You must have a driving licence to drive on public roads. To get a driving licence you must pass a test. There are many driving schools where you can learn with the help of a qualified instructor.

You get a full driving licence in three stages:

1 Apply for a provisional licence. You need this licence while you are learning to drive. With this you are allowed to drive a motorcycle up to 125cc or a car. You must put L plates on the vehicle, or D plates in Wales. Learner drivers cannot drive on a motorway. If you drive a car, you must be with someone who is over 21 and who has had a full licence for over three years. You can get an application form for a provisional licence from a post office.
2 Pass a written theory test.
3 Pass a practical driving test.

Drivers may use their licence until they are 70. After that the licence is valid for three years at a time.

In Northern Ireland, a newly-qualified driver must display an R-plate (for registered driver) for one year after passing the test.

Overseas licences

If your driving licence is from a country in the European Union (EU), Iceland, Liechtenstein or Norway, you can drive in the UK for as long as your licence is valid.

If you have a licence from a country outside the EU, you may use it in the UK for up to 12 months. During this time you must get a UK provisional driving licence and pass both the UK theory and practical driving tests, or you will not be able to drive after 12 months.

Insurance

It is a criminal offence to have a car without proper motor insurance. Drivers without insurance can receive very high fines. It is also illegal to allow someone to use your car if they are not insured to drive it.

Road tax and MOT

You must also pay a tax to drive your car on the roads. This is called road tax. Your vehicle must have a road tax disc which shows you have paid. You can buy this at the post office. If you do not pay the road tax, your vehicle may be clamped or towed away.

If your vehicle is over three years old, you must take it every year for a Ministry of Transport (MOT) test. You can do this at an approved garage. The garage will give you an MOT certificate when your car passes the test. It is an offence not to have an MOT certificate. If you do not have an MOT certificate, your insurance will not be valid.

Safety

Everyone in a vehicle should wear a seat belt. Children under 12 years of age may need a special booster seat. Motorcyclists and their passengers must wear a crash helmet (this law does not apply to Sikh men if they are wearing a turban). It is illegal to drive while holding a mobile phone.

Speed limits

For all cars and motorcycles the speed limits are:

30 miles per hour (mph) in built-up areas, unless a sign shows a different limit

60 mph on single carriageways

70 mph on motorways and dual carriageways

101
everyday needs (from
Life in the UK)
06

Speed limits are lower for buses, lorries and cars pulling caravans.

It is illegal to drive when you are over the alcohol limit or drunk. The police can stop you and give you a test to see how much alcohol you have in your body. This is called a breathalyser test. If a driver has more than the permitted amount of alcohol (called being 'over the limit') or refuses to take the test, he or she will be arrested. People who drink and drive can expect to be disqualified from driving for a long period.

Accidents

If you are involved in a road accident:

- don't drive away without stopping – this is a criminal offence
- call the police and ambulance on 999 or 112 if someone is injured
- get the names, addresses, vehicle registration numbers and insurance details of the other drivers
- give your details to the other drivers or passengers and to the police
- make a note of everything that happened and contact your insurance company as soon as possible.

Note that if you admit the accident was your fault, the insurance company may refuse to pay. It is better to wait until the insurance company decides for itself whose fault the accident was.

Identity documents

At present, UK citizens do not have to carry identity (ID) cards. The government is, however, making plans to introduce them in the next few years.

Proving your identity

You may have to prove your identity at different times, such as when you open a bank account, rent accommodation, enrol for a college course, hire a car, apply for benefits such as housing benefits, or apply for a marriage certificate. Different organisations may ask for different documents as proof of identity. These can include:

- official documents from the Home Office showing your immigration status
- a certificate of identity

- a passport or travel document
- a National Insurance (NI) number card
- a provisional or full driving licence
- a recent gas, electricity or phone bill showing your name and address
- a rent or benefits book.

Check that you understand:

- How films are classified
- Why you need a television licence
- The rules about the selling and drinking of alcohol
- How to get a driving licence
- What you need to do to be allowed to drive a vehicle in the UK
- What you should do if you have an accident
- When you might have to prove your identity, and how you can do it

---

Test yourself

Now that you have studied this section, go to page 156 to find the practice questions that refer to this material and check that you have understood all the information.

If you have any problems with answering the questions about this section you should read through it again, paying particular attention to the areas pointed out in the 'Check that you understand' boxes.

✳ ✳

Summary

This is the first of two chapters of the official material that concentrate on the more day-to-day aspects of UK society. Where the previous three chapters have looked at government organisations and how the UK is made up in terms of ethnicity, population and religion, this section examines how to buy or rent accommodation, what local authorities do and how to look after your health, children's education and your finances by accessing the services that are available. Understanding these things is essential in order to live a successful life in the UK.

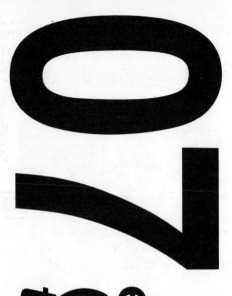

07

employment (from *Life in the UK*)

In this chapter you will:
- find out about how to look for work and how to apply for jobs
- see how people's rights and responsibilities in employment work
- learn about childcare while you are working and about how children are protected in employment.

Overview

This final chapter of official material covers a very important area of life in the UK – that of employment. There is information about how to look for and apply for jobs and training and about the discrimination laws in the UK. It also covers the more technical aspects of employment such as written contracts, tax and National Insurance, so you should make sure that you understand these areas.

This is a very useful chapter if you are employed or looking for work, and there are many sources of help, advice and support given here. If you can understand and remember this material you will be in a better position in your working life as well as on the way to passing your British Citizenship Test.

What this chapter does not cover is whether you are entitled to work in the UK or not. That is the job of the Home Office and can be a complicated subject, so you should check with the authorities if you are unsure.

Now on to the official information that comes from Chapter 6: Employment, in the Home Office publication *Life in the United Kingdom – A Journey to Citizenship*.

****

In this chapter there is information about:

- Looking for work and applying for jobs
- Training and volunteering
- Equal rights and discrimination
- Rights and responsibilities at work
- Working for yourself
- Childcare and children at work

Looking for work

If you are looking for work, or are thinking of changing your job, there are a number of ways you can find out about work opportunities. The Home Office provides guidance on who is allowed to work in the UK. Not everyone in the UK is allowed to work and some people need work permits, so it is important to check your status before taking up work. Also, employers have to check that anyone they employ is legally entitled to work in the UK. For more information and guidance, see the

Home Office website 'Working in the UK' – **www.working intheuk.gov.uk**.

Jobs are usually advertised in local and national newspapers, at the local Jobcentre and in employment agencies. You can find the address and telephone number of your local Jobcentre under Jobcentre Plus in the phone book or see: **www.jobcentreplus. gov.uk** Some jobs are advertised on supermarket notice boards and in shop windows. These jobs are usually part-time and the wages are often quite low. If there are particular companies you would like to work for, you can look for vacancies on their websites.

Jobcentre Plus is run by a government department – the Department for Work and Pensions. Trained staff give advice and help in finding and applying for jobs as well as claiming benefits. They can also arrange for interpreters. Their website **www.jobcentreplus.gov.uk** lists vacancies and training opportunities and gives general information on benefits. There is also a low cost telephone service – Jobseeker Direct, 0845 60 60 234. This is open 9 a.m. to 6 p.m. on weekdays and 9 a.m. to 1 p.m. on Saturdays.

Qualifications

Applicants for some jobs need special training or qualifications. If you have qualifications from another country, you can find out how they compare with qualifications in the UK at the National Academic Recognition Information Centre (NARIC), **www.naric.org.uk**.

For further information contact UK NARIC, ECCTIS Ltd, Oriel House, Oriel Road, Cheltenham, Glos, GL50 1XP, telephone: 0870 990 4088, email: info@naric.org.uk.

Applications

Interviews for lower paid and local jobs can often be arranged by telephone or in person. For many jobs you need to fill in an application form or send of a copy of your curriculum vitae (CV) with a covering letter or letter of application.

A covering letter is usually a short letter attached to a completed application form, while a letter of application gives more detailed information on why you are applying for the job and why you think you are suitable. Your CV gives specific details on your education, qualifications, previous employment, skills and interests. It is important to type any letters and your CV on a computer or word processor as this improves your chance of being called for an interview.

Employers often ask for the names and addresses of one or two referees. These are people such as your current or previous employer or college tutor. Referees need to know you well and to agree to write a short report or reference on your suitability for the job. Personal friends or members of your family are not normally acceptable as referees.

Interviews

In job descriptions and interviews, employers should give full details of what the job involves, including the pay, holidays and working conditions. If you need more information about any of these, you can ask questions in the interview. In fact, asking some questions in the interview shows you are interested and can improve your chance of getting the job.

When you are applying for a job and during the interview, it is important to be honest about your qualifications and experience. If an employer later finds out that you gave incorrect information, you might lose your job.

Criminal record

For some jobs, particularly if the work involves working with children or vulnerable people, the employer will ask for your permission to do a criminal record check. You can get more information on this from the Home Office Criminal Records Bureau (CRB) information line, telephone 0870 90 90 811. In Scotland, contact Disclosure Scotland: **www.disclosurescotland. co.uk** Helpline: 0870 609 6006.

Training

Taking up training helps people improve their qualifications for work. Some training may be offered at work or you can do courses from home or at your local college. This includes English language training. You can get more information from your local library and college or from websites such as **www.worktrain.gov.uk** and **www.learndirect.co.uk**. Learndirect offers a range of online training courses at centres across the country. There are charges for courses but you can do free starter or taster sessions. You can get more information from their free information and advice line 0800 100 900.

Volunteering and work experience

Some people do voluntary work and this can be a good way to support your local community and organisations which depend on volunteers. It also provides useful experience that can help with future job applications. Your local library will have information about volunteering opportunities.

You can also get information and advice from websites such as: **www.do-it.org.uk www.volunteering.org.uk** and **www.justdo something.net**.

Check that you understand:

- The Home Office provides guidance on who is entitled to work in the UK
- NARIC can advise on how qualifications from overseas compare with qualifications from the UK
- What CVs are
- Who can be a referee
- What happens if any of the information you have given is untrue
- When you need a CRB check
- Where you can find out about training opportunities and job seeking
- Benefits of volunteering in terms of work experience and community involvement

---

Test yourself

Now that you have studied this section, go to page 157 to find the practice questions that refer to this material and check that you have understood all the information.

If you have any problems with answering the questions about this section you should read through it again, paying particular attention to the areas pointed out in the 'Check that you understand' box.

Equal rights and discrimination

It is against the law for employers to discriminate against someone at work. This means that a person should not be refused work, training or promotion or treated less favourably because of their:

- sex
- nationality, race, colour or ethnic group
- disability
- religion
- sexual orientation
- age.

In Northern Ireland, the law also bans discrimination on grounds of religious belief or political opinion.

The law also says that men and women who do the same job, or work of equal value, should receive equal pay. Almost all the laws protecting people at work apply equally to people doing part-time or full-time jobs.

There are, however, a small number of jobs where discrimination laws do not apply. For example, discrimination is not against the law when the job involves working for someone in their own home.

You can get more information about the law and racial discrimination from the Commission for Racial Equality. The Equal Opportunities Commission can help with sex discrimination issues and the Disability Rights Commission deals with disability issues. Each of these organisations offers advice and information and can, in some cases, support individuals. From October 2007 their functions will be brought together in a new Commission for Equality and Human Rights. You can get more information about the laws protecting people at work from the Citizens Advice Bureau website: **www.adviceguide.org.uk**.

In Northern Ireland, the Equality Commission provides information and advice in respect of all forms of unlawful discrimination.

The Commission for Racial Equality, St Dunstan's House, 201-211 Borough High Street, London, SE1 1GZ, telephone: 020 7939 000, fax: 020 7939 0001, **www.cre.gov.uk**.

The Equal Opportunities Commission, Arndale House, Arndale Centre, Manchester M4 3EQ, telephone: 0845 601 5901, fax: 0161 838 8312, **www.eoc.org.uk**.

The Disability Rights Commission, DRC Helpline, FREEPOST MID02164, Stratford upon Avon CV37 9BR, telephone: 08457 622 633, fax: 08457 778 878, **www.drc.org.uk**.

The Equality Commission for Northern Ireland, Equality House, 7-9 Shaftesbury Square, Belfast BT2 7DP, telephone: 028 90 500600, **www.equalityni.org**.

Sexual harassment

Sexual harassment can take different forms. This includes:

- indecent remarks
- comments about the way you look that make you feel uncomfortable or humiliated
- comments or questions about your sex life
- inappropriate touching or sexual demands
- bullying behaviour or being treated in a way that is rude, hostile, degrading or humiliating because of your sex.

Men and women can be victims of sexual harassment at work. If this happens to you, tell a friend, colleague or trade union representative and ask the person harassing you to stop. It is a good idea to keep a written record of what happened, the days and times when it happened and who else may have seen or heard the harassment. If the problem continues, report the person to your employer or a trade union. Employers are responsible for the behaviour of their employees while they are at work. They should treat complaints of sexual harassment very seriously and take effective action to deal with the problem. If you are not satisfied with your employer's response, you can ask for advice and support from the Equal Opportunities Commission, your trade union or the Citizens Advice Bureau.

At work

Both employers and employees have legal responsibilities at work. Employers have to pay employees for the work that they do, treat them fairly and take responsible care for their health and safety. Employees should do their work with reasonable skill and care and follow all reasonable instructions. They should not damage their employer's business.

A written contract or statement

Within two months of starting a new job, your employer should give you a written contract or statement with all the details and conditions for your work. This should include responsibilities, pay, working hours, holidays, sick pay and pension. It should also include the period of notice that both you and your employer should give for the employment to end. The contract or written statement is an important document and is very useful if there is ever a disagreement about your work, pay or conditions.

Pay, hours and holidays

Your pay is agreed between you and your employers. There is a minimum wage in the UK that is a legal right for every employed person above the compulsory school leaving age. The compulsory school leaving age is 16, but the time in the school year when 16-year-olds can leave school in England and Wales is different from that in Scotland and Northern Ireland.

There are different minimum wage rates for different age groups. From October 2006 the rates are as follows:

- for workers aged 22 and above – £5.35 an hour
- for 18–21-year-olds – £4.45 an hour
- for 16–17-year-olds – £3.30 an hour.

Employers who pay their workers less than this are breaking the law. You can get more information from the Central Office of Information Directgov website, **www.direct.gov.uk** which has a wide range of public service information. Alternatively, you can telephone the National Minimum Wage Helpline, telephone: 0845 600 0678.

Your contract or statement will show the number of hours you are expected to work. Your employer might ask you if you can work more hours than this and it is your decision whether or not you do. Your employer cannot require you to work more hours than the hours agreed on your contract.

If you need to be absent from work, for example if you are ill or you have a medical appointment, it is important to tell your employer as soon as you can in advance. Most employees who are 16 or over are entitled to at least four weeks' paid holiday every year. This includes time for national holidays. Your employer must give you a pay slip, or a similar written statement, each time you are paid. This must show exactly how much money has been taken off for tax and national insurance contributions.

Tax

For most people, tax is automatically taken from their earnings by the employer and paid directly to HM Revenue and Customs, the government department responsible for collecting taxes. If you are self-employed, you need to pay your own tax. Money raised from income tax pays for government services such as roads, education, police and the armed forces. Occasionally HM Revenue and Customs sends out tax return forms which ask for full financial details. If you receive one, it is important to complete it and return the form as soon as possible. You can get help and advice from the HM Revenue and Customs self-assessment helpline, on: 0845 300 45 55.

More information

Tax allowances (how much you can earn before you are taxed) and tax rates (the percentage tax that will be taken from any income over your tax allowance) are decided each year according to government policy and requirements. They are then announced in the Budget by the Chancellor of the Exchequer in the House of Commons in March.

National Insurance

Almost everybody in the UK who is in paid work, including self-employed people, must pay National Insurance (NI) contributions. Money raised from NI contributions is used to pay contributory benefits such as the State Retirement Pension and helps fund the National Health Service. Employees have their NI contributions deducted from their pay by their employer every week or month. People who are self-employed need to pay NI contributions themselves: Class 2 contributions, either by direct debit or every three months and Class 4 contributions on the profits from their trade or business. Class 4 contributions are paid alongside their income tax. Anyone who does not pay enough NI contributions will not be able to receive certain benefits, such as Jobseeker's Allowance or Maternity Pay, and may not receive a full state retirement pension.

Getting a National Insurance number

Just before their 16th birthday, all young people in the UK are sent a National Insurance number. This is a unique number for each person and it tracks their National Insurance contributions.

Refugees whose asylum applications have been successful have the same rights to work as any other UK citizen and to receive a National Insurance number. People who have applied for asylum and have not received a positive decision do not usually have permission to work and so do not get a National Insurance number.

You need a National Insurance number when you start work. If you do not have a National Insurance number, you can apply for one through Jobcentre Plus or your local Social Security Office. It is a good idea to make an appointment by telephone and ask which documents you need to take with you. You usually need to show your birth certificate, passport and Home Office documents allowing you to stay in the country. If you need information about registering for a National Insurance number, you can telephone the National Insurance Registrations Helpline on 0845 91 57006 or 0845 91 55670.

Pensions

Everyone in the UK who has paid enough National Insurance contributions will get a State Pension when they retire. The State Pension age for men is currently 65 years of age and for women it is 60, but the State Pension age for women will increase to 65 in stages between 2010 and 2020. You can find full details of the State Pension scheme on the State Pension website, **www.thepensionservice.gov.uk** or you can phone the Pension Service Helpline: 0845 60 60 265.

In addition to a State Pension, many people also receive a pension through their work and some also pay into a personal pension plan too. It is very important to get good advice about pensions. The Pensions Advisory Service gives free and confidential advice on occupational and personal pensions. Their helpline telephone number is 0845 601 2923 and their website address is **www.opas.org.uk** Independent financial advisers can also give advice but you usually have to pay a fee for this service. You can find local financial advisers in the Yellow Pages and Thomson local guides or on the internet at **www.unbiased.co.uk**.

Health and safety

Employers have a legal duty to make sure the workplace is safe. Employees also have a legal duty to follow safety regulations and to work safely and responsibly. If you are worried about health and safety at your workplace, talk to your supervisor, manager or trade union representative. You need to follow the right procedures and your employer must not dismiss you or treat you unfairly for raising a concern.

Trade unions

Trade unions are organisations that aim to improve the pay and working conditions of their members. They also give their members advice and support on problems at work. You can choose whether to join a trade union or not and your employer cannot dismiss you or treat you unfairly for being a union member.

You can find details of trade unions in the UK, the benefits they offer to members and useful information on rights at work on the Trades Union Congress (TUC) website, **www.tuc.org.uk**.

Problems at work

If you have problems of any kind at work, speak to your supervisor, manager, trade union representative or someone else with responsibility as soon as possible. If you need to take any action, it is a good idea to get advice first. If you are a member of a trade union, your representative will help. You can also contact your local Citizens Advice Bureau (CAB) or Law Centre. The national Advisory, Conciliation and Arbitration Service (ACAS) website, **www.acas.org.uk** gives information on your rights at work. ACAS also offers a national helpline, telephone: 08457 47 47 47.

Losing your job and unfair dismissal

An employee can be dismissed immediately for serious misconduct at work. Anyone who cannot do their job properly, or is unacceptably late or absent from work, should be given a warning by their employer. If their work, punctuality or attendance does not improve, the employer can give them notice to leave their job.

It is against the law for employers to dismiss someone from work unfairly. If this happens to you, or life at work is made so difficult that you feel you have to leave, you may be able to get compensation if you take your case to an Employment Tribunal. This is a court which specialises in employment matters. You normally only have three months to make a complaint.

If you are dismissed from your job, it is important to get advice on your case as soon as possible. You can ask for advice and information on your legal rights and the best action to take from your trade union representative, a solicitor, a Law Centre or the Citizens Advice Bureau.

Redundancy

If you lose your job because the company you work for no longer need someone to do your job, or cannot afford to employ you, you may be entitled to redundancy pay. The amount of money you receive depends on the length of time you have been employed. Again your trade union representative, a solicitor, a Law Centre or the Citizens Advice Bureau can advise you.

Unemployment

Most people who become unemployed can claim Jobseeker's Allowance (JSA). This is currently available for men aged 18-65 and women aged 18–60 who are capable of working, available for work and trying to find work. Unemployed 16- and 17-year-olds may not be eligible for Jobseeker's Allowance but may be able to claim a Young Person's Bridging Allowance (YPBA) instead. The local Jobcentre Plus can help with claims. You can get further information from the Citizens Advice Bureau and the Jobcentre Plus website: **www.jobcentreplus.gov.uk**.

New Deal

New Deal is a government programme that aims to give unemployed people the help and support they need to get into work. Young people who have been unemployed for 6 months and adults who have been unemployed for 18 months are usually required to join New Deal if they wish to continue receiving benefit. There are different New Deal schemes for different age groups. You can find out more about New Deal on 0845 606 2626 or: **www.newdeal.gov.uk**.

The government also runs work-based learning programmes which offer training to people while they are at work. People receive a wage or an allowance and can attend college for one day a week to get a new qualification.

You can find out more about the different government schemes, and the schemes in your area, from Jobcentre Plus, **www.jobcentreplus.gov.uk**, or your local Citizens Advice Bureau.

Working for yourself

Tax

Self-employed people are responsible for paying their own tax and National Insurance. They have to keep detailed records of what they earn and spend on the business and send their business accounts to HM Revenue and Customs every year. Most self-employed people use an accountant to make sure they pay the correct tax and claim all the possible tax allowances.

As soon as you become self-employed you should register yourself for tax and National Insurance by ringing the HM Revenue and Customs telephone helpline for people who are self-employed, on 0845 915 4515.

Help and advice

Banks can give information and advice on setting up your own business and offer start-up loans, which need to be repaid with interest. Government grants and other financial support may be available. You can get details of these and advice on becoming self-employed from Business Link, a government-funded project for people starting or running a business – **www.businesslink. gov.uk** telephone: 0845 600 9 006.

Working in Europe

British citizens can work in any country that is a member if the European Economic Area (EEA). In general, they have the same employment rights as a citizen of that country or state.

Check that you understand:

Equal rights

- the categories covered by the law and exceptions
- equal job/equal pay regardless of gender
- the different commissions working to promote equal opportunities
- the grounds for sexual harassment complaints

At work

- the importance of contracts of employment
- the minimum wage and holiday entitlement
- information that has to be provided on pay slips

Tax

- what is deducted from your earnings and why
- the difference between being self-employed and employed
- where to get help if you need it when filling out forms
- the purpose of National Insurance and what happens if you don't pay enough contributions
- how you can get a National Insurance number

Pensions

- who is entitled to a pension
- what age men and women can get a pension

Health and safety

- employer and employee obligations
- what to do if you have concerns about health and safety

Trade Unions

- what they are and who can join

Losing your job

- where to go if you need advice on a problem at work
- possible reasons for dismissal
- the role of Employment Tribunals
- who can help
- the timescale for complaining
- entitlement to redundancy pay

Self-employment

- responsibility for keeping detailed records and paying tax and national insurance
- the role of Business Link

Test yourself

Now that you have studied this section, go to page 157 to find the practice questions that refer to this material and check that you have understood all the information.

If you have any problems with answering the questions about this section you should read through it again, paying particular attention to the areas pointed out in the 'Check that you understand' box.

Childcare and children at work

New mothers and fathers

Women who are expecting a baby have a legal right to time off work for antenatal care. They are also entitled to at least 26 weeks' maternity leave. These rights apply to full-time and part-time workers and it makes no difference how long the woman has worked for her employer. It is, however, important to follow the correct procedures and to give the employer enough notice about taking maternity leave. Some women may also be entitled to maternity pay but this depends on how long they have been working for their employer.

Fathers who have worked for their employer for at least 26 weeks are entitled to paternity leave, which provides up to two weeks' time off from work, with pay, when the child is born. It is important to tell your employer well in advance.

You can get advice and more information on maternity and paternity matters from the personnel officer at work, your trade union representative, your local Citizens Advice Bureau, the Citizens Advice Bureau website **www.adviceguide.org.uk** or the government website **www.direct.gov.uk**.

Childcare

It is Government policy to help people with childcare responsibilities to take up work. Some employers can help with this. The ChildcareLink website **www.childcarelink.gov.uk** gives information about different types of childcare and registered childminders in your area, or telephone 08000 96 02 96.

Hours and time for children at work

In the UK there are strict laws to protect children from exploitation and to make sure that work does not get in the way of their education. The earliest legal age for children to do paid work is set at 14. There are a few exceptions that allow children under the age of 14 to work legally and these include specific work in performing, modelling, sport and agriculture. In order to do any of this work it is necessary to get a licence from the local authority.

By law, children aged 14 to 16 can only do light work. There are particular jobs they are not allowed to do and these include delivering milk, selling alcohol, cigarettes or medicines, working in a kitchen or a chip shop, working with dangerous machinery or doing any other kind of work that might cause them any kind of injury. Children who work have to get an employment card from their local authority and a medical certificate of fitness for work.

The law sets out clear limits for the working hours and times for 14–16-year-old children. Every child must have at least two consecutive weeks a year during the school holidays when they do not work. They cannot work:

- for more than 4 hours without a one-hour rest break
- for more than 2 hours on any school day or a Sunday
- before 7 a.m. or after 7 p.m.
- for more than one hour before school starts
- for more than 12 hours in any school week.

15 and 16-year-olds can work slightly more hours than 14-year-olds on a weekday when they are not at school, on Saturdays and in school holidays. The local authority has a duty to check that the law is obeyed. If it believes that a young person is working illegally, it can order that the young person is no longer employed. You can find more information on the TUC website, **www.worksmart.org.uk**.

Check that you understand:

Maternity and paternity rights
- entitlement to maternity leave and pay for both part-time and full-time workers
- paternity leave entitlement
- the importance of following the right procedures and providing sufficient notice

Children at work
- minimum age for starting work
- jobs 14- to 16-year-olds are not allowed to do
- the maximum hours allowed
- requirements – medical certificate and employment card
- the local authority's responsibility for protecting children

Test yourself

Now that you have studied this section, go to page 157 to find the practice questions that refer to this material and check that you have understood all the information.

If you have any problems with answering the questions about this section you should read through it again, paying particular attention to the areas pointed out in the 'Check that you understand' box.

* *

Summary

This final section of the official *Life in the UK* material deals with something that it is essential to understand if living in the UK – employment. Knowing where to find information about job vacancies, where to go for help if you have problems at work and how to get a National Insurance number are all important parts of life in the UK.

08

practice questions and answers

In this chapter you will:
- have the opportunity to check your knowledge of the Home Office material
- find timed tests to do in order to find out if you can work under conditions similar to those in the actual test
- be able to assess your chances of passing the British Citizenship Test.

Overview

This is a very important part of this book and an equally important part of your preparation for the test. If you work your way through these practice questions you will undoubtedly improve your understanding of the material that you have to learn and will also be able to check your progress and assess when you are ready for the test. There are plenty of questions to test your knowledge, and three complete tests that you can do to time so that, as far as possible, you can recreate the test conditions and check that you are able to answer the required number of questions in the time allowed.

The test

First, let's have a reminder of the format of the test. It will consist of 24 questions for which you are allowed 45 minutes. This is plenty of time to think carefully about each of your answers and to go back and check any answers that you are uncertain about. As we said briefly in Chapter 2, the questions will be asked in a variety of ways:

- In the first type of question, four possible answers will follow the question. This is a 'multiple choice' question and you must choose what you think is the correct answer.
- You will be given a statement about some aspect of the material and you must decide whether it is true or false.
- You must be extra careful with this third type of question. You will be given four statements – two are correct and two are not – and you must select the two that are right. You must select the correct number of options, i.e. two. If you try to answer this type of question with one option, three options or four options, your answer will not be correct.
- The last type of question is also one you should be careful with. You will be given two statements – one will be right and one will be wrong and, of course, you must select the one that is correct.

Before you start the actual test, you will be given the opportunity to do a practice test using the computer. The results of this will not affect your actual test results so it is definitely worthwhile to take the time to do this practice. It will enable you to see exactly how the computer test works and will help you to settle down and give your very best performance when you do the test for real.

It is essential that you work carefully through the test. The computer will indicate which questions you have answered, so even if you do not know the answer to a question immediately you can go back to it when you have finished the rest of your answers. It is a good idea too, if you find you have time to spare, to go back through your answers, checking to see that you have not made any careless mistakes.

Practice questions

As you will see, the practice questions are grouped together according to the section of the material to which they refer, so you will be able to work through the material and test yourself on each section as you go. If you get a question wrong, look back to the appropriate section and try again.

After the section of practice questions there are three complete tests, with 24 questions each and with questions randomly chosen from all the sections – just like in the real test. After you have completed all the practice questions and are satisfied that you understand the material, it is a good idea to do the complete tests to time, keeping to exam conditions as much as possible – i.e. try to do them when you will not be interrupted, in a quiet room and allow yourself 45 minutes with a clock or watch handy so that you can keep an eye on the time. After each complete test you can check your results and will be able to see if you are ready for your test. If you get 18 or more right in each of the timed tests you will be ready to tackle the real thing.

The answers to all these questions and tests are at the end of this chapter for easy checking.

A changing society

Migration to Britain

Q1 Which of these statements is correct?

a Britain is a nation of immigrants.

b Most Britons come from Asia.

Q2 Where did many Irish labourers work when they came to Britain? Select the correct answer.

a on the buses

b on farms

c in factories

d on canals and railways

Q3 Which of these statements is correct?

a There was a famine in Ireland in the 17th century.

b There was a famine in Ireland in the mid-1840s.

Q4 Which of these statements is correct?

a Large numbers of Jewish people came to Britain to escape racist attacks.

b Very few Jewish people came to Britain to escape racist attacks.

Migration since 1945

Q5 When was the invitation by the British government to come to Britain extended to people from the West Indies?

a in the 1970s

b in the 1950s

c 1945

d 1948

Q6 Which two industries sent agents to find workers in India and Pakistan in the 1950s?

a transport

b textiles

c engineering

d catering

Q7 Why did immigration to Britain decrease in the late 1960s?

a Because workers did not want to come to Britain.

b Because the British government passed new laws restricting immigration.

c Because there was no housing for them.

d Because everyone who wanted to settle here had already come.

Q8 From which two places did approximately 50,000 refugees arrive in Britain in the 1970s?

a Uganda

b India

c South East Asia

d Pakistan

The changing role of women

Q9 Which two of these statements is correct?

a Women did not have the right to vote in the early 1850s.

b In the early 1950s women were allowed to vote when they reached 30.

c Men and women had equal rights in the 19th century.

d Women's earnings belonged to their husbands for most of the 19th century.

Q10 Is the statement below true or false?

Pre-1857 a married woman had a right to divorce her husband.

a True

b False

Q11 Which of these statements is correct?

a In the late 19th and early 20th centuries women started to campaign for greater rights, including the right to vote.

b In the late 19th and early 20th women were happy with the rights they had.

Q12 Why did women decrease their protests for greater rights?

a They became fed up with the campaign.

b They won the rights they had campaigned for.

c Women joined the war effort.

d Their husbands told them to stop.

Q13 Which of these statements is correct?

a After the First World War women won only the right to vote.

b After the First World War women won the right to vote and to stand for Parliament.

Q14 At what age were women able to vote after their rights were changed at the end of the First World War?

a 21

b 30

c 18

d 25

Q15 During which two years were women's right to vote changed?

a 1914

b 1918

c 1928

d 1945

Q16 Is the statement below true or false?
During the first few decades of the 20th century women were sometimes asked to leave work when they married.

a True
b False

Q17 Which two rights were given to women during the 1970s?
a to have an abortion
b to become an MP
c not to be discriminated against by employers on the grounds of sex
d to receive equal pay

Women in Britain today

Q18 Is the statement below true or false?
Women make up slightly less than half of the workforce.

a True
a False

Q19 Which two of these statements are correct?
a Women continue to be employed in traditionally female areas.
b Women are doing a much wider range of work than before.
c Attitudes to the work women should do will not change.
d Women's employment areas have narrowed.

Q20 Who has the main responsibility for housework and childcare in British homes today?
a children
b men
c women
d household jobs are shared equally

Q21 Which two of these statements are correct?
a More needs to be done to achieve equality.
b Women in Britain have the same access to promotion as men have.
c Women do not have equality in the workplace.
d A woman is as likely as a man to get a better-paid job.

Children, family and young people

Q22 Is the statement below true or false?
Children and young people under 19 make up almost a quarter of the UK population.

a True
b False

Q23 Which of these two statements is correct?
a Young people live with their families well into adulthood.
b Many young people move away from their families when they reach adulthood.

Q24 Is the statement below true or false?
Most children receive weekly pocket money from their parents.
a True
b False

Q25 Which of these two statements is correct?
a Children in the UK play mainly outside the home.
b Children in the UK do not play outside as much as they used to.

Q26 Which two of these statements are correct?
a There is no evidence that incidents of child molestation are increasing.
b Children are in more danger today than they used to be.
c Stories of child molestation are often reported in newspapers.
d There is less concern for child safety today than 50 years ago.

Q27 Why have family patterns in Britain changed in the past 20 years?
a Because the cost of living has increased.
b Because of changing attitudes towards divorce and separation.
c Because children are naughtier.
d Because of legislation that has been passed.

Q28 What proportion of children live in families with just one parent?
a one-third
b 10%
c almost 25%
d over a half

Education

Q29 Is the statement below true or false?
Testing of pupils at ages 7, 11 and 14 is compulsory in England.
a True
b False

Q30 Which of these two statements is correct?
a Education in the UK is compulsory from the ages of 5 to 16 (4 to 16 in Northern Ireland).
b Education in the UK is compulsory from the ages of 5 to 18 (4 to 18 in Northern Ireland).

Q31 What examination is usually taken by pupils in England and Wales at the age of 16?
a SATs
b A levels
c GCSEs
d A/S levels

Q32 Which two of these statements are correct?
a Many young people take A/S and A levels at 16.
b A/S and A levels are usually taken before GCSEs.
c Many young people take A/S and A levels at 17 and 18.
d A/S and A levels are usually taken after GCSEs.

Work

Q33 Which two of these statements are correct?
a It is common for young people to have a part-time job while they are still at school.
b Children are always supported by their parents, so have no need to work.
c Children are not allowed to work while they are still at school.
d It is estimated that there are two million children at work at any one time.

Q34 Is the statement below true or false?
The most common jobs for children are newspaper delivery and work in supermarkets and newsagents.
a True
b False

Q35 Which of these two statements is correct?

a Parents do not like their children to work.

b Many parents believe that part-time work helps children to become more independent.

Q36 Is the statement below true or false?

Young people over 16 are allowed to purchase alcohol.

a True

b False

Q37 How is the problem of alcohol abuse being tackled in Britain?

a The age at which young people can buy alcohol is being raised.

b Pubs and clubs are being asked not to serve anyone under 20.

c Penalties are increasing, including on-the-spot fines.

d The amount of alcohol that young people can buy is being limited.

Q38 Is the statement below true or false?

Half of young adults have used illegal drugs.

a True

b False

Q39 Which two of these statements are correct?

a There is no proven link between hard drugs and crime.

b Crack cocaine and heroin are not hard drugs.

c There is a well-established link between hard drugs and crime.

d Drug misuse carries a huge social and financial cost to the country.

Young people's political and social attitudes

Q40 What reason have researchers given for the low first-time voter activity in the 2001 general election?

a lack of knowledge of the political process

b laziness

c lack of interest in the political process

d inability to get to a voting station

Q41 At what age are young people able to vote in elections in Britain?

a 20

b 16

c 21

d 18

Q42 What proportion of young people questioned in a survey had taken part in some form of community activity in the past year?

a less than half

b over 80%

c one quarter

d 10%

UK today: a profile

Population

Q43 What was the recorded population of the UK in 2005?

a Over 60 million

b Just under 50 million

c 55 million

d Just under 60 million

Q44 Which two of these statements are correct?

a Wales has the smallest proportion of the population of the UK.

b England has the largest proportion of the population of the UK.

c Northern Ireland has the smallest proportion of the population of the UK.

d Scotland has the largest proportion of the population of the UK.

Q45 Is the statement below true or false?

The population of Wales is nearly 5 million.

a True

b False

Q46 Which area(s) of the UK have seen a decline in population over the last 20 years?

a the South and South-East

b Scotland

c the North-East and North-West

d Wales

Q47 Is the statement below true or false?
The UK population has grown by 7.7% since 1971.

a True

b False

Q48 Which two of these statements are correct?

a Britain has an ageing population.

b People aged 60 and over form a smaller part of the population than children under 16.

c People aged 60 and over form a larger part of the population than children under 16.

d There has been a general decrease in population in the UK over the last 20 years.

The census

Q49 Which of these two statements is correct?

a The next census will be in 2011.

b The next census will be in 2012.

Q50 The only year a census was not taken was 1941. Why was this?

a Insufficient people sent their forms back.

b It was forgotten.

c Britain was at war.

d It was decided that the information would not be useful.

Q51 Which two of these statements are correct?

a Every household receives a census form.

b There is free choice about whether or not to complete the census form.

c Only households in certain areas receive a census form.

d The census form must, by law, be completed.

Q52 Which of these two statements is correct?

a Information about individuals from the census is published immediately.

b Information about individuals is anonymous and confidential.

Ethnic diversity

Q53 What is the largest ethnic minority in Britain?

a Black Caribbean

b Black African

c Indian

d Bangladeshi

Q54 Which two of these statements are correct?

a People of mixed race make up almost 10% of the UK population.

b People of Chinese descent number 2 million of the UK population.

c People of Pakistani descent make up 1.3% of the UK population.

d The UK population is 92% white.

Q55 Which of these two statements is correct?

a There are more Black African people than Black Caribbean people among the UK population.

b There are more Indian people than people of Bangladeshi descent in the UK population.

Q56 According to the 2001 census, how many Indian people are there in the UK population?

a 0.6 million

b 0.2 million

c 1.1 million

d 0.1 million

Q57 Which two of these statements are correct?

a Approximately 10% of ethnic minorities live in Wales.

b Most members of ethnic minorities live in England.

c Members of ethnic minority groups make up 9% of the total population of England.

d Most members of ethnic minorities live in Scotland.

Q58 Which of these two statements is correct?

a More than 5% of ethnic minorities live in Wales and Scotland combined

b Less than 1% of ethnic minorities live in Northern Ireland

Q59 Is the statement below true or false?

Forty-five per cent of the ethnic minorities live in the London area.

a True

b False

The nations and regions of the UK

Q60 Which of these two statements is correct?

a The distance from the north coast of Scotland to the south-west corner of England is about 320 miles.

b The distance from the north coast of Scotland to the south-west corner of England is about 870 miles.

Religion

Religions in the UK

Q61 Which two of these statements are correct?

a Britain is historically a Christian society.

b Everyone in Britain has to follow a Christian religion.

c Everyone in Britain has a right to religious freedom.

d Britain historically does not have any religion.

Q62 Is the statement below true or false?

The majority of the UK population said that they had a religion in the 2001 census.

a True

b False

Q63 Which two of these statements are correct?

a The largest religion after Christian was Jewish.

b The largest religion after Buddhists were Sikhs.

c Nearly 3% of the population described their religion as Muslim.

d One per cent of the population described their religion as Hindu.

Q64 Which of these two statements is correct?

a The majority of people in Britain who have a religious belief regularly attend services.

b Only a minority of the people in Britain with a religious belief regularly attend services.

Q65 Is the statement below true or false?

A greater proportion of people in Scotland than in England attend Church.

a True

b False

The Christian Churches

Q66 What is the Church of England also known as?

a The Main Church

b The Anglican Church

c The State Church

d The Number One Church

Q67 Which two of these statements are correct?

a The King or Queen holds the title of Supreme Governor of the Church of England.

b Only a king can be Supreme Governor – not a queen.

c The Church of England came into existence in the 18th century.

d The monarch is the head of the Church of England.

Q68 Which of these two statements is correct?

a Heirs to the throne can marry anyone of any religion.

b Heirs to the throne are not allowed to marry anyone who is not Protestant.

Q69 Is the statement below true or false?

The Archbishop of York is the spiritual leader of the Church of England.

a True

b False

Q70 In practice, who chooses the Archbishop of Canterbury?

a The King or Queen

b The current Archbishop of Canterbury

c The Prime Minister

d Other senior Church officers

Q71 Which two of these statements are correct?

a The Presbyterian denomination does not exist in the UK today.

b There is no established church in Wales or Northern Ireland.

c Baptist, Presbyterian and Quakers denominations all exist today.

d Twenty-five per cent of Christians in the UK are Roman Catholic.

Q72 Which of these two statements is correct?

a In Scotland the established church is the Catholic Church.

b In Scotland the established church is the Presbyterian Church.

Q73 Is the statement below true or false?
Over half of the population of Northern Ireland is Roman Catholic.

a True

b False

Patron saints

Q74 Which of these two statements is correct?

a St. Andrew is the patron saint of England.

b St. Andrew is the patron saint of Scotland.

Q75 Is the statement below true or false?
In Britain, only Scotland takes its national day as an official holiday.

a True

b False

Q76 Is the statement below true or false?
St. David's day is the 1 March.

a True

b False

Q77 Is the statement below true or false?
Public holidays are called Bank Holidays.

a True

b False

Customs and traditions

Festivals

Q78 Which of these two statements is correct?

a The Notting Hill Carnival is held in London.

b The Notting Hill Carnival is held in Edinburgh.

The main Christian festivals

Q79 When is the birth of Jesus Christ celebrated?

a 1 January

b Easter

c 25 December

d New Year

Q80 Which Christian festivals are the most celebrated in the UK?

a Christmas and Easter

b Ascension Day and St. George's Day

c St. Valentine's Day and Christmas

d St. David's Day and Easter

Q81 Which two of these statements are correct?

a Christmas is a public holiday.

b Christmas is a normal working day.

c Christmas is for people of the Christian faith only.

d Christmas is celebrated by both Christians and non-Christians.

Q82 What religious traditions and festivals are children taught about in school?

a only the Christian traditions

b just Jewish and Christian festivals

c only Christmas and Easter

d various festivals from religions including Muslim, Hindu and Jewish

Q83 What do most British families eat on Christmas Day?

a roast beef and Yorkshire pudding

b fish and chips

c sirloin steak

d turkey

Q84 Which of these two statements is correct?

a Many families attend a church service on Christmas Eve or on Christmas morning.

b Churches are usually closed on Christmas Day.

Q85 Which of these two statements is correct?

a Father Christmas is shown in pictures as an old man with a beard.

b Father Christmas is shown in pictures as a slim young man.

Q86 Which of these two statements is correct?

a Boxing Day is the day after Easter.

b Boxing Day is the day after Christmas.

Other festivals and traditions

Q87 When is Remembrance Day?

a 1 January

b 11 March

c 11 May

d 11 November

Q88 Which of these two statements is correct?

a Children dress up at Hallowe'en and play 'trick or treat'.

b Hallowe'en commemorates a plot to bomb the Houses of Parliament.

Q89 Is the statement below true or false?

New Year celebrations in the UK start on 31 December.

a True

b False

Q90 Which two of these statements are correct?

a In Scotland, New Year can be a bigger festival than Christmas.

b Christmas is far more important in Scotland than New Year.

c In Scotland New Year is also called Hogmanay.

d New Year is not celebrated in Scotland.

Q91 Which two of these statements are correct?

a Mother's Day is celebrated three weeks before Easter.

b Only young children give flowers and chocolates to their mothers on Mother's Day.

c Mother's Day is celebrated on the Sunday before Easter.

d On Mother's Day children of all ages give their mothers gifts of flowers or chocolates.

Q92 Which of these two statements is correct?

a On April Fool's Day people play jokes on each other until 12 midnight.

b On April Fool's Day people play jokes on each other until 12 noon.

Q93 Which two of these statements are correct?

a A group of Baptists are said to have been behind the Gunpowder Plot.

b The Gunpowder Plot is commemorated today by giving gifts and sending cards.

c A group of Catholics are said to have been behind the Gunpowder Plot.

d The Gunpowder Plot is commemorated today with fireworks.

Q94 Is the statement below true or false?

Many people wear artificial poppies in their buttonholes on Remembrance Day.

a True

b False

Q95 How is Guy Fawkes Night usually celebrated in the UK?

a People give gifts to their family and friends.

b People set off fireworks.

c People send cards to all their friends.

d A two-minute silence is held.

Sport

Q96 Which two of these statements are correct?

a Most people do not watch or take part in any sporting activities.

b Sport plays a major part in many people's lives.

c There are no United Kingdom teams for football or rugby.

d Very few sports are played in Britain.

Q97 Which of these two statements is correct?

a The Grand National is a tennis tournament.

b The FA Cup Final is a football match.

How the United Kingdom is governed

The British Constitution

Q98 Is the statement below true or false?
A country's constitution is always written down.
a True
b False

Q99 Which of these two statements is correct?
a The UK is a constitutional democracy.
b The UK is a dictatorship.

The monarchy

Q100 Who is the Head of State of the United Kingdom?
a the Prime Minister
b Queen Elizabeth II
c Prince Charles
d the Archbishop of Canterbury

Q101 Is the statement below true or false?
Britain is the only European country with a constitutional monarchy.
a True
b False

Q102 Which of these two statements is correct?
a The King or Queen can only 'advise, warn, and encourage' the government.
b The King or Queen has a duty to speak out against government policy.

Q103 What title does the heir to the throne hold?
a Duke of Edinburgh
b Princess Royal
c Prince of Wales
d Prince Consort

Q104 What does the Queen read at the beginning of a new parliamentary session?
a the latest bestselling novel
b a speech summarising the government's policies for the year ahead
c the Chancellor's speech
d a speech written by her husband, the Duke of Edinburgh

Government

Q105 Is the statement below true or false?
The party with the largest number of MPs forms the government.
a True
b False

Q106 Which two of these statements are correct?
a Britain's system of government is a dictatorship.
b Voters in certain constituencies elect more MPs than others.
c MPs work in the House of Commons.
d Voters in each constituency elect their MP.

The House of Commons

Q107 Is the statement below true or false?
The House of Commons is more important than the House of Lords.
a True
b False

Q108 How many parliamentary constituencies are there?
a 400
b 568
c 646
d 246

Elections

Q109 How often are Parliamentary elections held to elect MPs in Britain?
a every year
b at least every three years
c at least every five years
d at least every ten years

Q110 Which of these two statements is correct?
a By-elections are held every five years.
b By-elections are held when an MP resigns or dies in office.

Q111 What sort of a system is used to elect Members of the House of Commons?
a greatest number of seats
b proportional representation
c first past the post
d a coalition

The Whips

Q112 What do the Whips do?

a They keep order during political debates.

b They assist the Prime Minister to answer questions.

c They are in charge of refreshments.

d They ensure discipline and attendance of MPs at voting time.

Q113 Which two of the following statements are correct?

a The Chief Whip often attends Cabinet meetings.

b The Chief Whip assists the Speaker in arranging a schedule of proceedings for the House of Commons.

c The Chief Whip decides when elections are called.

d The Chief Whip has an automatic right to attend the House of Lords.

European parliamentary elections

Q114 How many seats are there in the European Parliament for representatives from the UK?

a 250

b 98

c 78

d 28

The House of Lords

Q115 Who or what can overrule the House of Lords regarding the passage of new laws?

a the Lord Chancellor

b the Queen

c the Prime Minister

d the House of Commons

Q116 Which two of these statements are correct?

a Life peers are appointed by the Prime Minister.

b Life peers are usually members of the Church of England.

c The House of Lords has the power to prevent the passage of new legislation.

d Life peers have usually had a professional career before becoming peers.

The Prime Minister

Q117 Which two of these statements are correct?

a Prime Ministers live at 10 Downing Street.

b The Prime Minister's residence is Buckingham Palace.

c The Prime Minister has just one close assistant.

d Prime Ministers have a country house called Chequers.

Q118 Select one of these two statements.

a The Prime Minister cannot be removed from office.

b The MPs of the governing party can remove the Prime Minister from office.

The Cabinet

Q119 Who become ministers in charge of government departments?

a anyone who wants to

b senior MPs

c new MPs

d MPs from minority parties

Q120 Which two of these statements are correct?

a The Prime Minister has no control over who is a member of the Cabinet.

b The Prime Minister is the leader of the party in power.

c The Prime Minister appoints ministers of state.

d The Prime Minister does not appoint Cabinet ministers.

Q121 Which two of these statements are correct?

a The Chancellor of the Exchequer is responsible for the economy.

b The Finance Secretary is responsible for the economy.

c The Home Secretary is responsible for law, order and immigration.

d The Minister for Law and Order is responsible for the justice system.

Q122 Which of these two statements is correct?

a All decisions are made independently by the Cabinet.

b Cabinet decisions on major matters are submitted to Parliament for approval.

Q123 Is the statement below true or false?

The Lord Chancellor is the minister responsible for legal affairs.

a True

b False

The Opposition

Q124 Which two of these statements are correct?

a The second largest party in the House of Commons opposes the government.

b The second largest party in the House of Commons cannot choose matters for discussion in Parliament.

c The second largest party in the House of Commons is called The Opposition.

d The second largest party in the House of Commons is always the Liberal Democrats.

Q125 Who is in the Shadow Cabinet?

a all the opposition MPs

b all the MPs in the second largest party in the House of Commons

c senior members of the main opposition party

d government ministers

The Speaker

Q126 Is the statement below true or false?

The Speaker of the House of Commons represents Parliament at ceremonial occasions.

a True

b False

Q127 Which two of these statements are correct?

a The Speaker represents the government.

b The Speaker is politically neutral.

c The speaker keeps order during political debates.

d The Speaker is appointed by the Opposition.

The party system

Q128 Is the statement below true or false?

MPs who do not represent any of the main political parties are called 'independents'.

a True

b False

Q129 How often do the political parties hold their policy-making conferences?

a every five years

b every week

c every month

d every year

Pressure and lobby groups

Q130 Which two of these statements are correct?

a Pressure groups are falling in popularity.

b Pressure groups are an increasingly important part of political life.

c The public are more likely to support a pressure group than to join a political party.

d Pressure groups are not allowed to represent economic interests.

The civil service

Q131 What helps to stop civil servants from becoming too politically involved?

a Civil servants are people who have no interest in politics.

b The government imposes penalties for political involvement.

c The chance of a General Election bringing another party to power.

d A lack of knowledge of the political process.

Devolved administration

Q132 Which of these two statements is correct?

a There has been devolved administration in Wales and Scotland since 1969.

b There has been devolved administration in Wales and Scotland since 1997.

The Welsh Assembly Government

Q133 Is the statement below true or false?

In the National Assembly for Wales the members may speak in either Welsh or English.

a True

b False

Q134 Which two of these statements are correct?

a Elections to the National Assembly of Wales are held every five years.

b The Welsh ministers have very little discretion in making regulations.

c The National Assembly of Wales is situated in Cardiff.

d The National Assembly of Wales has the power to make decisions on important matters such as education and health services.

Q135 How many members does the National Assembly of Wales have?

a 40

b 60

c 80

d 100

The Parliament of Scotland

Q136 How many Members of the Scottish Parliament are there?

a 129

b 130

c 219

d 229

Q137 Is the statement below true or false?

The Parliament of Scotland is situated in Glasgow.

a True

b False

Q138 Which two of these statements are correct?

a Power in the Scottish Parliament is shared between the Liberal Democrats and the Conservatives.

b The Scottish Parliament uses a 'first past the post' system.

c Power in the Scottish Parliament is often shared between the Liberal Democratic and Labour parties.

d Members of the Scottish Parliament are elected by a form of proportional representation.

The Northern Ireland Assembly

Q139 How many elected members does the Northern Ireland Assembly have?

a 98

b 100

c 105

d 108

Q140 Why has the Northern Ireland Assembly been set up with a system of proportional representation?

a to ensure power sharing

b to give more seats to the Protestants

c to avoid a two-party system

d to give them a change from the first-past-the-post system

Local government

Q141 When are local elections held?

a January

b March

c April

d May

Q142 Which two of these statements are correct?

a Local councils are often referred to as local authorities.

b Local councils have to provide 'mandatory services' as decided by central government.

c Local councils decide for themselves what services they will provide.

d Local authorities have more control over the organisation of their services than they did in the past.

Q143 Is the statement below true or false?

Most of the money for local authority services comes from the Council Tax.

a True

b False

The judiciary

Q144 Is the statement below true or false?

Judges have the task of applying the Human Rights Act.

a True

b False

Q145 Which of these two statements is correct?

a Judges have to interpret the law.

b The government may overrule judges' interpretation of their laws.

Q146 Who decides who is guilty or innocent of serious crimes?

a a judge

b a jury

c a magistrate

d a lawyer

The police

Q147 Which two of these statements are correct?

a The largest police force in Britain is the Metropolitan Police.

b The government can have any individual arrested.

c The police investigate serious complaints against themselves.

d The police have operational independence.

Non-departmental public bodies

Q148 Which of these two statements is correct?

a Semi-independent agencies set up by the government are also known as 'quickies'.

b Non-departmental public bodies go by the nickname of 'quangos'.

The role of the media

Q149 Is the statement below true or false?

The press in Britain is free from government control.

a True

b False

Q150 Which two of these statements are correct?

a Copies of Hansard are available in large libraries.

b Hansard is a private document restricted to MPs.

c Only the Prime Minister may read Hansard.

d Hansard is reproduced on the internet.

Q151 Which of these two statements is correct?

a Most people receive their political information from Hansard.

b Most people receive their political information from newspapers, TV and radio.

Q152 Which two of these statements are correct?

a Editors of most newspapers hold strong political opinions.

b Editors of newspapers must put their own opinions to one side.

c Editors run campaigns to influence government policy.

d Editors are unable to influence government policy.

Q153 Is the statement below true or false?

Rival political viewpoints are given equal time on radio and television at election periods.

a True

b False

Who can vote?

Q154 Which of these two statements is correct?

a The UK has had a fully democratic system from 1918.

b The UK has had a fully democratic system from 1928.

Q155 When was the present voting age of 18 set?

a 1918

b 1928

c 1969

d 1971

Q156 Is the statement below true or false?

The electoral register is updated in May every year.

a True

b False

Q157 Which of these two statements is correct?

a By law, each local authority has to make the electoral register available to members of the public.

b The electoral register is a confidential document.

Standing for office

Q158 What is the minimum age to be eligible to stand for public office?

a 16

b 18

c 21

d 25

Q159 Which of these two statements is correct?

a To become a local councillor it is not necessary to have a local connection.

b To become a local councillor it is necessary to have a local connection.

Contacting elected members

Q160 Which of these two statements is correct?

a You can contact your MP by letter or phone at their constituency office or at the House of Commons.

b If you want to contact your MP you must go to the House of Commons.

How to visit Parliament and the Devolved Administrations

Q161 Which of these two statements is correct?

a The general public are not allowed inside Parliament.

b The general public can visit Parliament by getting tickets from their MP or by queuing at the public entrance.

Q162 Is the statement below true or false?

Guided tours of the Welsh Assembly are available.

a True

b False

Q163 Which two of these statements are correct?

a Only people from Northern Ireland may visit Stormont.

b It is not possible to visit Stormont.

c You can arrange a visit to Stormont by contacting the Education Service.

d You can arrange a visit to Stormont by contacting an MLA.

Q164 Which of these two statements is correct?

a Scottish Parliament Members are called MSPs.

b Scottish Parliament Members are called SPMs.

The UK in Europe and the world

The Commonwealth

Q165 Which two of these statements are correct?

a The Commonwealth contains over 20 billion people.

b The Prime Minister is Head of the Commonwealth.

c The Commonwealth has a membership of 53 states.

d The Queen is the head of the Commonwealth.

The European Union

Q166 What was the reason behind the formation of the European Union?

a to make things difficult for non-members

b to make a profit for its members

c to reduce the likelihood of another European war

d to give jobs to bureaucrats

Q167 Which two of these statements are correct?

a Britain was a founder member of the European Economic Community.

b Britain joined the European Union in 1973.

c The European Union was set up by six Western European countries.

d Britain was keen to join the European Union right from the start.

Q168 Which of these two statements is correct?

a The regulations imposed to allow free movement of people, goods and service have always been popular.

b One of the main aims of the EU today is for member states to become a single market.

Q169 Is the statement below true or false?

Citizens of EU member states have the right to travel to or work in other EU countries.

a True

b False

Q170 What is another name for the Council of the European Union?

a The Council of Europe

b The European Union

c The European Economic Community

d The Council of Ministers

Q171 Which of these two statements is correct?

a The European Parliament meets in London.

b The European Parliament meets in Strasbourg and Brussels.

Q172 Where is the European Commission based?

a Strasbourg

b Paris

c Brussels

d London

The Council of Europe

Q173 Is the statement below true or false?

The Council of Europe draws up conventions and charters.

a True

b False

The United Nations

Q174 What is the main function of the UN Security Council?

a to debate world poverty

b to recommend action in the event of international crises and threats to peace

c to form a single market throughout the world

d to recommend how countries can change their laws

Everyday needs

Housing

Q175 Which of these statements is correct?

a Most people in the UK own their own home.

b Most people in the UK live in rented accommodation.

Q176 Is the statement below true or false?

Mortgages are usually short-term loans.

a True

b False

Q177 Who does an estate agent usually represent?

a the government

b the seller of a house

c the buyer of a house

d the local authority

Q178 Which two of these statements are correct?

a The system for buying a house is the same throughout the UK.

b The offer on a house is always legally binding as soon as it is made.

c In most of the UK a buyer makes an offer on a house 'subject to contract'.

d In Scotland the seller of a house sets a price and buyers make offers over that amount.

Q179 Which of these statements is correct?

a Housing provided by local authorities is often called 'council housing'.

b Local authorities do not provide housing.

Q180 Is the statement below true or false?

A tenancy agreement explains the conditions of renting a property.

a True

b False

Q181 What is the purpose of the deposit paid at the beginning of a tenancy?

a to pay the first year's rent

b as extra money for the landlord

c to cover the cost of any damage

d as a contribution towards furnishing the property

Q182 Which two of these statements are correct?

a A landlord cannot raise the rent during your tenancy without your agreement.

b A tenancy agreement is usually for an indefinite period.

c An inventory tells you about your tenancy.

d A landlord cannot force a tenant to leave.

Q183 Which of these statements is correct?

a A landlord can choose his tenant on whatever basis he wishes.

b It is unlawful for a landlord to discriminate against someone looking for accommodation.

Q184 Which of these statements is correct?

a The Citizens Advice Bureau will advise on housing problems.

b You must consult the local authority about housing problems.

Services in and for the home

Q185 Is the statement below true or false?

Water can be paid for in one payment or in instalments.

a True

b False

Q186 How can you recycle your rubbish at home?

a Only garden rubbish can be recycled.

b Recycling at home is not possible in the UK.

c Put it all in the bin.

d Separate paper, glass and so on from other rubbish for collection.

Q187 Which two items are paid for partly by Council Tax?

a central government costs

b police

c education

d state pensions

Q188 Which of these statements is correct?

a Nothing can be done about neighbours who cause a nuisance.

b Neighbours who cause serious problems can be evicted from their home.

Money and credit

Q189 Is the statement below true or false?

The euro is used throughout the European Union.

a True

b False

Q190 What do you need to open a bank or building society account?

a lots of money

b a loan

c documents to prove your identity

d a credit card

Q191 Which two of these statements are correct?

a A store card is like a credit card but used only in a specific shop.

b The interest on credit and store cards can be very high.

c Credit cards can help you to stay out of debt.

d You can draw money from your bank account using a credit card.

Q192 Which of these statements is correct?

a Travel insurance will pay for your holiday.

b Travel insurance is useful if you lose your luggage.

Q193 Is the statement below true or false?

The UK's system of social security pays benefits to everyone.

a True

b False

Health

Q194 What do you usually need in order to register with a GP?

a a credit card

b a debit card

c a store card

d a medical card

Q195 Select two of these statements.

a No one pays for prescriptions in the UK.

b Prescriptions are free to everyone aged 60 or over.

c Anyone over 18 has to pay for prescriptions.

d You should take a prescription to a pharmacy.

Q196 Which of these statements is correct?

a You can see a nurse by telephoning NHS Direct.

b If you have an out-of-hours medical emergency you should ring 999 or 112.

Q197 Is the statement below true or false?

NHS Direct is a 24-hour telephone information service.

a True

b False

Q198 Where are eye tests free in the UK?

a England

b Wales

c Scotland

d Northern Ireland

Q199 Select two of these statements.

a Dental treatment is free for most people.

b All dentists in the UK work for the NHS.

c Most people have to pay for dental treatment.

d A dentist will explain the charges before treatment begins.

Q200 Which of these statements is correct?

a When you are pregnant you receive support from a GP and from a midwife.

b Most women in the UK have their babies at home.

Q201 Is the statement below true or false?
Both parents must register a baby's birth.

a True

b False

Education

Q202 At what age do children attend primary school in England and Wales?

a 5 to 12 years

b 5 to 11 years

c 4 to 11 years

d 11 to 16 years

Q203 Which two of these items do parents have to pay for in secondary schools?

a tuition

b school uniforms

c science experiments

d school outings

Q204 Which of these statements is correct?

a Parents are rarely school governors.

b Parents are always represented on a school's governing body.

Q205 Is the statement below true or false?
Courses for adults over 18 are always offered at primary schools.

a True

b False

Q206 At what age can young people leave school?

a 15 years

b 11 years

c 18 years

d 16 years

Q207 Which two of these statements are correct?

a Everyone over 16 must pay for courses at Further Education colleges.

b Most courses at Further Education colleges are free up to the age of 19.

c Young people may be able to get financial help with studies when they leave school at 16.

d There is no financial help with education available after the age of 16.

Q208 Which of these statements is correct?

a Students do not usually contribute to their costs at university.

b When students start work after university they must pay back student loans.

Leisure

Q209 Is the statement below true or false?

Film classification 18 means that no one under 18 is allowed to see or rent the film.

a True

b False

Q210 Who can get a free television licence in the UK?

a everyone

b anyone over 18

c anyone over 65

d anyone over 75

Q211 What sort of driving licence do you get when you are learning to drive?

a a nominal licence

b a theory licence

c a provisional licence

d a full licence

Q212 Which of these statements is correct?

a People who drink and drive will only be fined.

b People who drink and drive can expect to be disqualified from driving.

Q213 Is the statement below true or false?

If you have an accident you can drive away and report it later.

a True

b False

Q214 Which two of these items could be used to prove identity?

a a photo of you and your family

b a recent gas, electricity or phone bill showing your name and address

c a letter from a friend

d a driving licence

Employment

Looking for work

Q215 What document would you send with a job application to give details of your education and experience?
a your old school reports
b a curriculum vitae (CV)
c copies of your qualification certificates
d a previous job description

Q216 Which of these statements is correct?
a Voluntary work is unpaid so there are no rewards.
b Voluntary work can give you useful work experience.

Equal rights and discrimination

Q217 Is the statement below true or false?
Employers are not allowed to treat someone less favourably because of their age.
a True
b False

Q218 On what extra grounds is discrimination banned in Northern Ireland?
a religious belief or political opinion
b weight
c height
d qualifications

Q219 In which two situations are men and women entitled to equal pay?
a when they work for the same company
b when they do the same job
c when they do work of equal value
d when they are working in the same department

Q220 Which of these statements is correct?
a Sexual harassment only applies to women.
b Sexual harassment can take different forms.

At work

Q221 Is the statement below true or false?

An employer should give an employee a written contract or statement within 30 days of starting work.

a True

b False

Q222 What is the minimum hourly rate (as at October 2006) for someone aged 18–21 years old?

a £5.35

b £5.00

c £4.45

d £3.30

Q223 Which two items of information must be shown on pay slips given to you by your employer?

a how much has been deducted for tax

b your hourly rate of pay

c your holiday entitlement

d the amount deducted for National Insurance

Q224 Which of these statements is correct?

a Most employees are entitled to five weeks' paid holiday per year.

b Most employees are entitled to four weeks' paid holiday per year, including national holidays.

Q225 Is the statement below true or false?

HM Revenue and Customs are responsible for collecting taxes.

a True

b False

Q226 Which of these items are the proceeds of National Insurance used for?

a maternity benefits

b contributory benefits

c public transport

d paying MPs salaries

Q227 Which two places or organisations can help you to get a National Insurance number?

a your local authority

b Jobcentre Plus

c your local Social Security Office

d your trade union

Q228 Which of these statements is correct?

a Both men and women receive a pension at the age of 60.

b Men cannot receive a state pension until they reach the age of 65.

Q229 Is the statement below true or false?

Employees have a legal duty to follow safety regulations.

a True

b False

Q230 For what can an employee be dismissed immediately?

a being late

b being off work sick

c incompetence

d serious misconduct

Q231 Which two types of records must self-employed people keep?

a details of what they spend on their business

b details of what they earn

c details of the hours they work

d details of their customers

Childcare and children at work

Q232 Which of these statements is correct?

a Women are entitled to 26 weeks off with pay when they have a baby.

b Women may be entitled to maternity leave with pay, depending on how long they have worked for their employer.

Q233 Is the statement below true or false?

Every child must have four weeks a year, during school holidays, when they do not work.

a True

b False

Q234 What is the minimum age at which a young person can start work?

a 13 years old

b 14 years old

c 15 years old

d 16 years old

Timed test 1

Q1 Select two correct statements.
a Protestant Huguenots came to Britain from France.
b Protestant Huguenots went from Britain to France in the 16th and 17th centuries.
c Protestant Huguenots came to Britain because of the weather.
d Protestant Huguenots came to Britain to escape religious persecution.

Q2 Is the statement below true or false?
The British Government encouraged workers to come to Britain to help to rebuild Britain.
a True
b False

Q3 Which of these statements is correct?
a There was a shortage of labour in the UK after the war.
b There was no shortage of labour in the UK after the war.

Q4 Is the statement below true or false?
Women took on a greater variety of work during the First World War.
a True
b False

Q5 Which of these two statements is correct?
a Women make up 51% of the workforce.
b Women make up 45% of the workforce.

Q6 Is the statement below true or false?
Employment opportunities for women are worse now than they have ever been.
a True
b False

Q7 What is seen as a reason for children not playing outside?
a Children are becoming lazier.
b Parents keep children inside to do chores.
c Children have too much homework.
d Home entertainment such as TV, videos and computers keeps them indoors.

Q8 What proportion of the population as a whole has used illegal drugs at one time or another?

a half

b one-third

c two-thirds

d one-quarter

Q9 Which of these two statements is correct?

a In the 2001 general election, the majority of first-time voters used their vote.

b In the 2001 general election, only one in five potential first-time voters cast their vote.

Q10 Which two of these statements are correct?

a A census of the UK population is taken every 5 years.

b The first census was taken in 1801.

c The first census was taken in 1901.

d A census of the UK population is taken every 10 years.

Q11 Is the statement below true or false?

About three-quarters of the African Caribbean, Pakistani, Indian and Bangladeshi communities were born in the UK.

a True

b False

Q12 Which two of these statements are correct?

a Both Wales and Scotland have their own language.

b Irish Gaelic is spoken in some parts of Scotland.

c Welsh is widely spoken in Wales.

d Scotland does not have its own language.

Q13 What date is St. Valentine's Day celebrated?

a 28 February

b 14 February

c 1 March

d 1 April

Q14 What is the official report on Parliamentary proceedings called?

a The Times

b Hansard

c Parliament Today

d The House of Commons

Q15 Which two of these statements are correct?

a Non-departmental government bodies are sometimes called quangos.

b Non-departmental bodies carry out a limited range of public duties.

c Non-departmental public bodies are independent organisations.

d Appointments to non-departmental government bodies are made by the Queen.

Q16 When was the Council of Europe created?

a 1973

b 1957

c 1949

d 2004

Q17 Which two of these statements are correct?

a The United Nations has 150 member countries.

b The UN was set up immediately after the First World War.

c The United Nations aims to promote international peace and security.

d The UN Security Council has 15 members.

Q18 What is a mortgage?

a a special loan from a bank or building society

b a statement supplied by a solicitor about a property

c a surveyor's report

d a contract to buy a house

Q19 Is the statement below true or false?

If you end a tenancy before the agreed time, you usually have to pay the rent for the agreed period of the tenancy.

a True

b False

Q20 Which of these two statements is correct?

a If only one person lives in a house, you get a 50% reduction in the Council Tax.

b If only one person lives in a house, you get a 25% reduction in the Council Tax.

Q21 What are credit unions?
a building societies
b financial co-operatives
c loan companies with high interest rates
d credit cards

Q22 Which of these two statements is correct?
a A GP can only treat physical illnesses.
b A GP can treat both mental and physical illnesses.

Q23 Which two of these statements are correct?
a Prescriptions are free for everyone.
b Prescriptions are free for anyone under 16 years of age.
c Prescriptions are free for anyone pregnant or with a baby under 12 months old.
d Prescriptions are free for anyone under 25 and in full-time education.

Q24 What is the minimum age someone is allowed to go into a betting shop?
a 14
b 16
c 18
d 21

Timed test 2

Q1 Which of these statements is correct?

a Any property or money a woman brought to marriage up to 1882 belonged to her husband.

b A man and his wife owned property jointly throughout the 19th century.

Q2 Approximately how many children and young people up to the age of 19 are there in Britain?

a 10 million

b 15 billion

c 15 million

d 5 million

Q3 Is the statement below true or false?

More than half of young people move on to higher education after school.

a True

b False

Q4 Which two of these statements are correct?

a Young people are often interested in specific political issues rather than in politics in general.

b Young people are not interested in any issues.

c Young people express strong concern about environmental issues and cruelty to animals.

d Young people are particularly interested in elections.

Q5 What proportion of all residents in the London area are members of ethnic minority groups?

a 50%

b 75%

c 19%

d 29%

Q6 Which two of these statements are correct?

a St. Andrew is the patron saint of Wales.

b St. George is the patron saint of England.

c St. Patrick's day is on 17 March.

d St. David is the patron saint of England.

Q7 Is the statement below true or false?

New Year is a Christian festival.

a True

b False

Q8 In what year did the Gunpowder Plot take place?

a 1705

b 1805

c 1516

d 1605

Q9 Which of these two statements is correct?

a The monarchy in Britain will be replaced with an elected President.

b The monarchy has important ceremonial roles.

Q10 Is the statement below true or false?

The Scottish Parliament and the Welsh Assembly have been set up with the same system of proportional representation.

a True

b False

Q11 Which of these two statements is correct?

a The key features of the civil service are party membership and efficiency.

b The key features of the civil service are political neutrality and professionalism.

Q12 Is the statement below true or false?

The UK has devolved power to regional administrations.

a True

b False

Q13 Where is the National Assembly for Wales situated?

a Wrexham

b Port Talbot

c Cardiff

d London

Q14 Is the statement below true or false?

The Commonwealth aims to promote democracy, good government and to eradicate poverty.

a True

b False

Q15 Why do decisions of the European Union have to be observed?

a Because the Europeans are always right.

b Because Parliament can't be bothered to argue.

c Because of wars in which we have fought.

d Because of the treaties that Britain has entered into.

Q16 Is the statement below true or false?

Housing Associations make large profits.

a True

b False

Q17 What type of charity is Shelter?

a a cancer research charity

b a hospice

c a housing charity

d an animal charity

Q18 Which of these two statements is correct?

a The cost of water usually depends on how much you use.

b The cost of water usually depends on the size of your property.

Q19 Is the statement below true or false?

People who do not have legal rights of settlement in the UK cannot usually receive benefits.

a True

b False

Q20 Which two of these statements are correct?

a Treatment from a GP is free.

b Unless you have exemption, you must pay for prescriptions.

c Vaccinations for foreign travel are free.

d You will always see your GP at his or her surgery and never at your home.

Q21 Which of the following two statements is correct?

a Independent schools are private schools.

b Independent schools are part of the state system.

Q22 Is the following statement true or false?

Boys and girls usually learn together in UK primary schools.

a True

b False

Q23 What sort of plates must a learner driver display in England, Scotland and Northern Ireland?

a D plates

b R plates

c L plates

d X plates

Q24 Which two of these statements are correct?

a UK citizens must carry identity cards at all times.

b UK citizens do not currently have to carry identity cards.

c The UK is planning to introduce identity cards.

d UK citizens must carry their passports at all times.

Timed test 3

Q1 Which two of these statements are correct?

a Women have achieved equal pay with men.

b Women's average hourly rate of pay is lower than it is for men.

c Women generally earn less than men.

d Women earn more than men overall.

Q2 Who gets better qualifications at school?

a boys

b boys and girls equally

c girls

d This has not been measured.

Q3 Is the statement below true or false?

Family patterns in Britain have remained unchanged in the last 20 years.

a True

b False

Q4 How do many young people delay starting their university course?

a by taking more exams

b by going back to school

c by taking a 'gap year'

d by learning a trade

Q5 Is the statement below true or false?

Only a quarter of young people questioned in a survey in 2003 had taken part in fund-raising or collecting money for charity.

a True

b False

Q6 Is the statement below true or false?

Census records can be consulted freely after 50 years.

a True

b False

Q7 In the 2001 census, which religion did seven out of ten people report they were?

a Muslim

b Christian

c Sikh

d Jewish

Q8 Which of these two statements is correct?

a Guy Fawkes led a plan to bomb the Houses of Parliament.

b It is not known who tried to bomb the Houses of Parliament.

Q9 Which of these two statements is correct?

a MPs all belong to the party in government.

b Most MPs belong to a political party.

Q10 How many politicians form the Cabinet?

a approximately 10

b approximately 15

c approximately 20

d approximately 30

Q11 Which of these two statements is correct?

a The Speaker chairs proceedings in the House of Commons.

b The Prime Minister chairs proceedings in the House of Commons.

Q12 Is the statement below true or false?

The present Queen has reigned for over 50 years.

a True

b False

Q13 Which two of these statements are correct?

a Until 1958 all peers were hereditary.

b There must be a general election every four years.

c There are 646 MPs elected by their constituencies.

d Most MPs are independent of political parties.

Q14 Which of these two statements is correct?

a The police service is organised locally.

b The police service is organised nationally.

Q15 Is the statement below true or false?

Approximately 20% of the funding for local government services comes from the collection of Council Tax.

a True

b False

Q16 Which two of these statements are correct?

a The UK has had a fully democratic system since 1969.

b Citizens of EU states can vote in all UK elections.

c The minimum voting age was changed to 18 in 1969.

d The UK has had a fully democratic system since 1928.

Q17 Is the statement below true or false?

In order to vote in elections you must have your name on the electoral register.

a True

b False

Q18 Who is responsible for collecting rubbish from residential properties?

a the landlord

b the insurance company

c the government

d the local authority

Q19 Is the following statement true or false?

Landlords should arrange insurance for rented buildings.

a True

b False

Q20 Who would you go to for advice about a loan?

a Citizens Advice Bureau

b a loan shark

c the government

d the local authority

Q21 Which two of these statements are correct?

a You must register a birth within six weeks.

b If the parents are married, either the mother or the father can register the birth.

c If the parents are not married, either the mother or the father can register the birth.

d Births are usually registered at the local community centre.

Q22 Which of these two statements is correct?

a Key Stage tests are also called 'the curriculum'.

b Key Stage tests are also called 'SATS'.

Q23 Is the following statement true or false?

Tickets for trains must usually be bought before you get on the train.

a True

b False

Q24 Which two of the following statements are correct?

a Tax must be sent monthly by cheque to HM Revenue and Customs.

b If you need a tax return you must ask for one.

c Most people have tax taken automatically from their earnings by their employer.

d Most people in paid work must pay National Insurance contributions.

Answers to practice questions

1.	a	41.	d
2.	d	42.	b
3.	b	43.	d
4.	a	44.	b and c
5.	d	45.	b
6.	b and c	46.	c
7.	b	47.	a
8.	a and c	48.	a and c
9.	a and d	49.	a
10.	b	50.	c
11.	a	51.	a and d
12.	c	52.	b
13.	b	53.	c
14.	b	54.	c and d
15.	b and c	55.	b
16.	a	56.	c
17.	c and d	57.	b and c
18.	a	58.	b
19.	a and b	59.	a
20.	c	60.	b
21.	a and c	61.	a and c
22.	a	62.	a
23.	b	63.	c and d
24.	a	64.	b
25.	b	65.	a
26.	a and c	66.	b
27.	b	67.	a and d
28.	c	68.	b
29.	a	69.	b
30.	a	70.	c
31.	c	71.	b and c
32.	c and d	72.	b
33.	a and d	73.	b
34.	a	74.	b
35.	b	75.	b
36.	b	76.	a
37.	c	77.	a
38.	a	78.	a
39.	c and d	79.	c
40.	c	80.	a

81. a and d
82. d
83. d
84. a
85. a
86. b
87. d
88. a
89. a
90. a and c
91. a and d
92. b
93. c and d
94. a
95. b
96. b and c
97. b
98. b
99. a
100. b
101. b
102. a
103. c
104. b
105. a
106. c and d
107. a
108. c
109. c
110. b
111. c
112. d
113. a and b
114. c
115. d
116. a and d
117. a and d
118. b
119. b
120. b and c
121. a and c
122. b
123. a

124. a and c
125. c
126. a
127. b and c
128. a
129. d
130. b and c
131. c
132. b
133. a
134. c and d
135. b
136. a
137. b
138. c and d
139. d
140. a
141. d
142. a and b
143. b
144. a
145. a
146. b
147. a and d
148. b
149. a
150. a and d
151. b
152. a and c
153. a
154. b
155. c
156. b
157. a
158. b
159. b
160. a
161. b
162. a
163. c and d
164. a
165. c and d
166. c

167. b and c
168. b
169. a
170. d
171. b
172. c
173. a
174. b
175. a
176. b
177. b
178. c and d
179. a
180. a
181. c
182. a and d
183. b
184. a
185. a
186. d
187. b and c
188. b
189. b
190. c
191. a and b
192. b
193. b
194. d
195. b and d
196. b
197. a
198. c
199. c and d
200. a
201. b
202. b
203. b and d
204. b
205. b
206. d
207. b and c
208. b
209. a

210. d
211. c
212. b
213. b
214. b and d
215. b
216. b
217. a
218. a
219. b and c
220. b
221. b
222. c
223. a and d
224. b
225. a
226. b
227. b and c
228. b
229. a
230. d
231. a and b
232. b
233. b
234. b

Answers to timed tests

Timed test 1

1. a and d
2. a
3. a
4. a
5. b
6. b
7. d
8. b
9. b
10. b and d
11. b
12. a and c
13. b
14. b
15. a and c
16. c
17. c and d
18. a
19. a
20. b
21. b
22. b
23. b and c
24. c

Timed test 2

1. a
2. c
3. b
4. a and c
5. d
6. b and c
7. b
8. d
9. b
10. b
11. b
12. a

13. c
14. a
15. d
16. b
17. c
18. b
19. a
20. a and b
21. a
22. a
23. c
24. b and c

Timed test 3

1. b and c
2. c
3. b
4. c
5. b
6. b
7. b
8. a
9. b
10. c
11. a
12. a
13. a and c
14. a
15. a
16. c and d
17. a
18. d
19. a
20. a
21. a and b
22. b
23. a
24. c and d

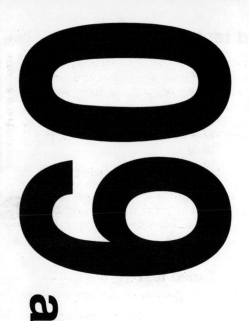

09

after your test

In this chapter you will:
- look at what happens after your test
- find out how to apply for your first British passport
- look at your rights and responsibilities as a new British citizen.

Introduction

After all the hard work of getting through the Citizenship Test is done, and with your Pass Notification Letter in hand, you may want to sit back and take it easy. But you still have some work to do. To take full advantage of your success in the test you must finish the job. Whether you are aiming for naturalisation or for settlement there are several forms to fill in and processes to go through.

If you are aiming to become a British citizen, these include:

- Citizenship Application Form (you will need your Pass Notification Letter for this – don't forget that if you lose this document you will have to sit the test again)
- Passport Application Form
- Welcoming Ceremony.

In addition, you may want to exercise your right to vote and to do that you will have to get yourself on the electoral register.

If you are applying for indefinite leave to remain, then the forms you will have to complete will depend entirely upon the circumstances of your stay here. Also, you should be aware that the forms and some of the rules covering settlement changed on 2 April 2007 and can change at any time so, to check your situation, get the correct forms and obtain up-to-date information, you are strongly advised to visit **www.ind.home office.gov.uk**.

This chapter will guide you through some of these essential forms and processes.

Applying for citizenship

If your ultimate goal is to obtain British citizenship, the first thing to do after passing your Citizenship Test – apart from celebrating – is to complete and submit your application. The application form – the AN Application for Naturalisation, as it is called (available from the Home Office website **www.ind.homeoffice.gov.uk**) – is 16 pages long and requires lots of different information, so you should set aside plenty of time and gather all your paperwork and personal details together before you start. If you are applying for indefinite leave to remain, there are different forms for you to complete.

The following items are all included in the Citizenship Application Form:

- personal details – name, address, date of birth, occupation and so on
- the name and address of anyone – such as a solicitor or immigration consultant – who will be representing you in your application
- your parents' personal details, including their dates and places of birth
- your children's details
- information about your marriage(s) – now and in the past: dates, names and places
- your Life in the UK Test results, including the test number – you will find this on your Pass Notification Letter
- all the UK addresses that you have lived at for the previous five years
- information about absences from the UK during the previous five years, including precise dates and the reasons why you were outside the UK – holidays, business trips, etc.
- details of your character referees – you will need to enter the names and addresses of two people who are prepared to give assurances as to your good character (i.e. character references); they should be over 25 and people who have known you well for some time, but they cannot be related to you
- full details of any criminal conviction (and you must submit notification immediately of any convictions or proceedings against you that occur while your application is being considered).

Note

If you and your wife or husband are applying for British citizenship at the same time, you both need to complete a separate form. A separate form must also be completed for all children and other family members applying for naturalisation.

When you have worked your way through all that, you must send it off together with:

- the appropriate fee – this is currently £655 (£735 for a husband and wife applying at the same time) – which includes the cost of your Welcoming Ceremony (levels of fees can be checked at **www.ind.homeoffice.gov.uk**)

- your Pass Notification Letter from your Life in the UK Test
- your passport.

By the time you get to this stage you will have done an enormous amount of work but may still feel unsure that you have included everything or have written all the information in the right place. You may therefore wish to use the Nationality Checking Service (NCS). Although there is a charge for this service – currently about £40 – it can save you money in the long term as there is no refund for incorrect applications. It can also be very handy if you are planning to go abroad during the period when your application is being checked as the checking service will photocopy your passport and return it to you before checking and sending off your application. They will check your application form to make sure you have completed it correctly and that all the supporting documentation you need has been attached. Incorrect completion of the forms is one of the top five reasons for applications for citizenship to fail (as we will see in the next section), so it is worthwhile spending the time and money to make sure that yours is absolutely perfect.

The National Checking Service is operated by local councils. To find your nearest participating council go to **www.lifeinthe uk.net/index.php/ncs**.

Finally, it is a good idea to take a photocopy of your completed form and documentation before you send them off. When you're ready, you should send your form, plus supporting documents, to:

The Home Office IND
Integrated Casework Directorate (Nationality)
Casework Support Unit
PO Box 12
Liverpool
L69 2UX
Telephone 0845 010 5200

Things that might go wrong

Lots of applications for citizenship fail. In many cases this is not because the people in question were not entitled to British citizenship but because they had not completed their application forms correctly or had misunderstood the requirements. In this section we will look at what can go wrong with your application and at how you might be able to avoid the problems.

The top five reasons for applications to be unsuccessful are:

- **The residency requirements are not met** – approximately four out of every ten applications fail because of problems regarding the residency requirement of five years (or three years for those married to a British citizen). It is important to be precise in all aspects of the details you put on your Citizenship Application Form. There are two areas where you need to pay special attention:

  i   Don't send your application too early. You must be sure that your date of entry to the UK is at least five years before the date of your application. You should have a date stamp from the Immigration Authorities as you entered the UK and this is the date you should use. So, for example, if your date stamp shows 2 May 2002 then the earliest you can apply for citizenship is 2 May 2007. If you haven't been in the UK for at least five years then your application will automatically be rejected – even if everything else is correct. You will also need to take into account any visa applications you have made while you're here (especially if you are applying for indefinite leave to remain) and the type(s) of visa you have held. If in doubt, ring the helpline before you submit your application.

  ii Check how long you have been absent from the UK in the previous five years. The rules about this are detailed and clear. You must not have been absent from the UK for more than 90 days in the 12 months immediately prior to the date of your application. Also, you must not have been absent for more than 450 days in the five years prior to your application. If your application is based on you being married to a British citizen, then you should not have been absent for more than 270 days in the three years prior to your application date.

- **The age or language requirements are not met** – nearly a third of applications fail for these two reasons. If you are under the age limit of 18 years then you cannot apply for British citizenship; if you are unable to display evidence of a sufficient grasp of the English language (via the Life in the UK Test) then your application will fail.

- **Problems with replying to Home Office enquiries** – during the period when your application is being considered you must make sure that you reply to all enquiries promptly. If you do not supply information additional to your application when requested, or if the immigration authorities are unable to contact you, then your application will fail.

- **The applicant is found to be not of good character** – extensive enquiries are carried out into an applicant's character and if these find any information which suggests that the applicant could be a threat to national security or that there is recurring criminal activity then the applicant will be deemed not suitable for British citizenship. These enquiries can involve the services of the police, HM Revenue and Customs (so make sure you've paid any tax you owe before you submit your application!), security services and various government agencies and may include a credit check.
- **The application has not been correctly completed** – the errors people make with their application forms include not enclosing the appropriate fee or mistakes with the supporting documents. Check your form thoroughly – make sure it is legible and that every single detail that you have entered on it is correct before you send it in. In addition, you can use the National Checking Service as detailed in the previous section.

If your application for British citizenship is refused (and if this is the case, then the Immigration and Nationality Directorate will give you a reason for the rejection), you may still reapply at a later date.

Applying for indefinite leave to remain

This is also known as settlement and there are separate forms for you to apply for this after you have passed the British Citizenship Test. The test is exactly the same whether you are ultimately intending to apply for citizenship or for settlement. If you are applying for indefinite leave to remain – i.e. making your permission to stay permanent rather than applying to simply extend your existing visa as you may have done in the past – there are lots of grounds on which you can apply. The form you will have to use will vary according to these grounds. For example, you may:

- hold a work permit and be highly skilled
- have lived in the UK for a long time
- be married to a person who has settled in the UK
- be in business here
- be an asylum seeker who currently has temporary leave to remain.

All of these situations demand specific forms if the person in that situation wishes to obtain indefinite leave to remain.

Copies of the forms (and guides to help you complete them) are available for download from the Home Office website – **www.ind.homeoffice.gov.uk**.

If, later, you decide to apply for citizenship, you will not need to take the British Citizenship Test again. Your Pass Notification Letter can be used for both settlement applications and naturalisation applications.

Top tip

If you are applying for indefinite leave to remain, you can use the application checking service offered by many local authorities in just the same way as if you were applying for naturalisation.

Staff will examine your application forms and supporting documents to make sure all is in order before you send them off.

Your Welcoming Ceremony (for new British citizens)

This is your big day! Your Welcoming Ceremony is the occasion when you are officially recognised as a new British Citizen. This is a relatively new addition to Britain – the government introduced the requirement from 1 January 2004 – but a ceremony to welcome new citizens is used in other countries such as Australia, the United States of America and Canada. The ceremony is part of the government's moves to make the process of becoming a British citizen more meaningful and celebratory and encouraging integration into British society.

Shortly after you've passed your test and sent your application forms with the appropriate fees and your Pass Notification Letter to the Home Office, you will receive notification from the Immigration and Nationality Directorate that you are being granted British citizenship. After this you have 90 days to attend a ceremony – attendance is compulsory, so make sure that you do so. Your local Register Office or Town Hall, where these ceremonies are usually held, will then send you an invitation to a ceremony.

More information

Make sure you attend your ceremony – if you don't, you will have to go through the whole application process again. You won't have to re-sit the British Citizenship Test, but you do have to pay the fees again, so not attending your ceremony could be an expensive mistake.

The ceremony itself will vary slightly from area to area, but the points listed below should give you a good idea of what to expect.

- It is a free occasion – the cost is included in the nationality application fee, so you don't have to pay any extra for the ceremony.
- You will be sent an invitation to take at least two guests with you to this very special occasion.
- It is a joint ceremony with others who are becoming British citizens. If you want a private ceremony, this is usually offered by local authorities at a charge so that you can take family and friends with you and make an extra special party of your ceremony.
- The ceremony is conducted by a Superintendent Registrar – this is the person who usually conducts weddings.
- There will be speeches by local dignitaries – the town's mayor or some other senior officer will often give a speech welcoming the new citizens. This is aimed at giving the ceremony a special, welcoming feel.
- You will say the oath of allegiance, in which you swear allegiance to the Crown and loyalty to your new country (see page 187). This is an important part of the ceremony and although you will not have to memorise the oath as the Registrar will read it out and you repeat it along with your fellow new citizens, you will probably feel more comfortable if you are familiar with it beforehand.
- You will be presented with a certificate stating that you are now a British citizen.
- Light refreshments may be provided on arrival.
- The National Anthem is usually played. Don't worry, you will not be expected to give a solo performance – or even to sing along with others if you don't want to – but it helps to know the words.

The National Anthem

God save our gracious Queen,
Long live our noble Queen,
God save the Queen,
Send her victorious,
Happy and glorious,
Long to reign over us,
God save the Queen.

- You will be given an information pack.
- You may even be given a small memento of the day and have your photograph taken – as a group or individually – to commemorate the day you became a British citizen.

It is important that you look after the certificate that you are given at your Welcoming Ceremony, as you will need to use it to obtain your first British passport – more about this in the following sections (see page 186).

What are your rights?

There is a variety of rights and privileges that are available to you when you become a British citizen, but these rights are not set down anywhere in one place. Unlike countries such as the United States of America, the United Kingdom does not have a written Bill of Rights. A Bill of Rights usually tells the citizens of a country what their rights are (such as freedom of speech or the freedom of assembly) and what the government is allowed to do. It will also set out how the judiciary must behave, punishments and right of appeal and so on.

Briefly, the main rights of a British citizen are:

- to hold a British Passport
- to vote in elections
- free medical treatment under the National Health Service
- free education for their children
- a variety of rights, privileges and protections conferred by laws passed by the government in areas such as consumer law, marriage and family law, the right of peaceful assembly and to privacy, freedom of speech plus fair treatment by the

courts and police, and a lack of discrimination on grounds of gender, ethnicity or age
- basic human rights as a result of Britain having signed up to the Convention on Human Rights.

Applying for a passport

Being able to obtain a British passport is one of the main benefits of becoming a British citizen. Some people consider a British passport to be superior to many others. It allows you to travel around the world, often, as is the case with the European Union, without having to obtain a visa. It can also serve as a perfect means of identification for all sorts of purposes.

Forms for applying for a UK passport are available from every post office. They are relatively simple to complete and ask for the following details:

- your personal details – name, address, date of birth and so on – and details of your parents
- the reference number and date of issue of your Naturalisation Certificate
- two countersigned photographs. The format for these photographs is strictly laid out in the documents that come with the application form. They must be two copies of a head and shoulders shot taken against a light grey, off-white or cream background, you must not be smiling and your face should not be in shadow. The size is also important – 35 mm wide and 45 mm high – and the position of your face is determined by the requirement that the distance between your chin and your crown must be between 29mm and 34mm high. Full instructions about these requirements will be included with the application form you obtain from a post office.

Your passport photographs must be countersigned. This means that a person of standing in the community (a police officer, solicitor, doctor, teacher or minister of religion, for example), who is a British or Irish passport holder, must sign one of the photographs on the back with the words 'I certify that this is a true likeness of (give your full name and title)' and the date.

Many people take these photographs with their own digital cameras, but the rules regarding the exact format and size of the photographs are very strict so this is not a recommended option unless you're very skilled with your camera. Passport photographs can be taken at the photo booths to be found in many post offices, supermarkets and shopping centres or, of course, taken by professional photographers.

Having obtained your passport form from a post office, it can also be a good idea to use the post office's 'check and send' service for passports. They currently charge £7 to examine your form and photographs so that any mistakes and problems can be spotted before you send the application to the passport agency. This can help to prevent your application being rejected for something simple that you may have missed.

The standard fee to obtain a first-time passport is currently £66 and should be sent with your application form.

Having obtained your photographs, filled in your form and had it checked you can now send it off. You should allow three weeks for delivery of your passport via the standard service, but there are quicker, more expensive levels of service available.

The UK Passport Agency runs a helpline for any problems you may encounter – 0870 521 0410.

Voting in elections

When you become a British citizen you acquire the right to vote in general, local and European parliamentary elections. Although you have this right to vote, it is not compulsory. If you don't want to exercise the right then no one can compel you to do so.

All British citizens can vote if:

• they are over 18 years old
• they are not in prison for a criminal offence
• they do not have a severe mental health problem
• their name appears on the electoral register.

Assuming that you fulfil the first three of these conditions, your next step is to get your name on the electoral register for your area. All councils collect the details of people in their area who are entitled to vote. Every year they deliver a form to every household and this must be completed with the details of everyone in the household who is entitled to vote. This form is also used to record details of people who may be called for jury service. If you do not return your form you may be prosecuted and be subject to a large fine – so if you receive one, fill it in and send it back straight away.

The electoral register forms are sent out every year so, if you want to, you can simply wait until one comes through your letterbox. Alternatively, you can get in touch with your local council to obtain a form. Either call in at the town hall or telephone to ask for a form to be sent to you.

Another voting right that you will gain as a British citizen is to vote in any other European Union country if you go to live there. Of course, you need to be registered to vote in that country to be able to exercise the right, but that is usually a simple matter. Alternatively, you can ignore the right to vote in that country and instead choose to continue to exercise your right in British elections.

Your responsibilities

The concept of responsibilities to go alongside the rights you obtain by becoming a British citizen is sometimes a difficult one to understand. The rights and benefits – the right to vote and to hold a British passport, to a free education or free medical treatment, for example – are quite clear, but the responsibilities are less obvious. The key to understanding your new responsibilities as a new British citizen is in the Oath of Allegiance. Here it is:

I (state your name) swear by Almighty God that, on becoming a British citizen, I will be faithful and bear true allegiance to Her Majesty Queen Elizabeth the Second, Her Heirs and Successors according to law.

I will give my loyalty to the United Kingdom and respect its rights and freedoms. I will uphold its democratic values. I will observe its laws faithfully and fulfil my duties and obligations as a British Citizen.

When you say these words at your Welcoming Ceremony you are taking on the responsibilities of a British citizen. Let's pick them out from the Oath of Allegiance. This is what you are promising:

- to be faithful and bear true allegiance to Her Majesty Queen Elizabeth the Second, Her Heirs and Successors according to law
- to be loyal to the United Kingdom

- to respect the country's rights and freedoms
- to uphold the United Kingdom's democratic values
- to observe its laws faithfully
- to fulfil your duties and obligations as a British citizen.

As you can see, these promises involve loyalty to and respect for the important institutions of the United Kingdom – the Monarchy, its democracy and legal systems. You are promising to obey laws and to behave with respect towards the things that are important in British society. The last one of these promises – to fulfil your duties and obligations as a British citizen – is vague, but successive governments have declared the need for British citizens to play their part in improving British society. It is thought that many of the problems in society today could be solved, or at least improved, by all citizens – both new and old – playing their part. This could mean an infinite variety of tasks that are seen as the responsibilities of citizenship, including helping others, charitable giving, bringing up children to be responsible citizens, consideration for others around us, taking care of our surroundings and voluntary work.

Getting involved in your community

If you have been living in the UK for many years and have settled down well, it is likely that you have already taken your place in your community. However, if you have not already done so, the time when you become a British citizen is an ideal time to think seriously about the part you can play.

Apart from voting in elections, there are many ways to get involved in your community. One of these is voluntary work and no matter where you live you will be able to find plenty of opportunities for helping other people in your area. Whatever your choice of voluntary work, it will be rewarding and is unlikely to be something that you will regret. If you start to look for voluntary work that you can do in your local area, you will be astounded by the choice that is out there. There are a number of websites (see the 'Useful organisations and websites' section at the back of this book for details) that will be able to give you plenty of contacts to start you off in your search for the perfect opportunity for you. Some websites even have the facility for you to enter your postcode and then you are given specific opportunities that are currently available very close to your home.

Summary

In this chapter we have dealt with some of the things that will happen in your life after you have passed your test. The most important of these is, of course, applying for British citizenship or settlement and we've gone through the processes for these applications as far as possible, bearing in mind that everyone's circumstances will be different. We've also considered some of the things that can go wrong with such applications and how you might be able to avoid problems. We've looked in some detail at the rights and responsibilities that come with citizenship, and how you can apply for a passport and get on the electoral register once you have just become a British citizen. In short, we've been looking at how you can make the most of a successful result in the Life in the UK Test and to continue to develop your own life in the UK.

Useful organisations and websites

www.lifeintheuktest.gov.uk – go to this website for lots of information about the test, including finding a test centre. You can also practise your computer skills and complete a practice test online.

Governmental offices

www.homeoffice.gov.uk/passports-and-immigration – plenty of advice about how to obtain a passport and about immigration

www.ind.homeoffice.gov.uk – Immigration and Nationality Directorate – part of the Home Office that deals specifically with immigration

For their Application Forms Unit, telephone 0870 241 0645 or download them from the website. For general enquiries about immigration call the Home Office's Immigration and Nationality Enquiry Bureau (INEB) on 0870 606 7766.

www.ukvisas.gov.uk – for advice and information about the complicated subject of visas

www.ukps.gov.uk – the UK Passport Service
UK Passport Service
Home Office
Immigration and Nationality Directorate
Lunar House
40 Wellesley Road
Croydon CR9 2BY

www.oisc.org.uk – the Office of the Immigration Services Commissioner. This website gives you a list of qualified immigration consultants and plenty of immigration advice.

www.ait.gov.uk – the Asylum and Immigration Tribunal. This is the organisation you should contact if you are denied leave to stay in the UK.

www.dwp.gov.uk – the Department of Work and Pensions. They will be able to advise on the benefits system.

Charitable organisations

www.iasuk.org – the Immigration Advisory Service. This is a charity providing advice about immigration and asylum law.

www.adviceguide.org.uk – the Citizens Advice Bureau website, with a section giving advice about immigration. They also have advice centres throughout Britain – you can find your nearest Citizens Advice office through this website.

Legal advice

www.ilpa.org.uk – Immigration Law Practitioners' Association

www.clsdirect.org.uk – Community Legal Services

www.legalservices.gov.uk – Legal Services Commissioner for advice about legal aid, if you are entitled to it

www.lawcentres.org.uk – Law Centres Federation

Learning English

www.englishuk.com English UK is the association for British Council accredited English language centres in the UK and their website contains details of privately owned schools, as well as state sector centres offering English courses.

www.learndirect.co.uk – provides lots of information about training courses, including those to improve your English

Refugee organisations

www.asylumsupport.info The National Asylum Support Service (NASS) may be able to give financial assistance for refugees who are destitute.

www.refugeecouncil.org.uk – gives advice to newly arrived refugees and asylum seekers in England (tel. 0207 3466777).

www.scottishrefugeecouncil.org.uk – gives advice to newly arrived refugees and asylum seekers in Scotland (tel. 0141 248 9799).

www.welshrefugeecouncil.org.uk – gives advice to newly arrived refugees and asylum seekers in Wales (tel. 029 20489800).

www.refugee-legal-centre.org.uk – provides legal representation for refugees and asylum seekers (tel. 0207 7803220).

Miscellaneous

www.nhsdirect.nhs.uk – the website for NHS Direct

www.do-it.org.uk – find a volunteering opportunity near you on this website

www.volunteer . . . k – promotes volunteering in England

www.volunte . . . .uk – promotes volunteering in Scotland

www.volur . . . s volunteering in Wales

www.volu . . . otes volunteering in Northern Ireland

www.csv . . . munity Service Volunteers organisation (CVS)

www.p . . . rk.gov.uk – useful site that allows you to enter y . . . nd find your nearest library

www.d . . . m – a directory of online dictionaries

www.ye . . . Pages online, to help you find all sorts of local . . . ent offices etc.

glossary

Here are some words that, if English is not your first language, you may not have come across before but that you need to know to be able to understand the materials and to help you to pass your citizenship test.

abolition The ending of something, such as a law or custom.

absent from work Not at work – maybe because of illness.

accountant Someone whose job is to keep and monitor financial and business records. They would often help a self-employed person to prepare tax records.

ageing population This is when the average age of a population is increasing. Causes for this include increasing life spans and falling birth rates.

Anglican Church Another name for the Church of England.

antenatal care The medical care given to a pregnant woman (and to her unborn baby).

April Fool's Day The 1 April every year, when people play jokes on one another.

Archbishop of Canterbury The head of the Church of England – selected by the Prime Minister. There are only two Archbishops in the Anglican Church – the Archbishop of Canterbury and the Archbishop of York.

Armed Forces The army, navy and air force, which defend a country.

arrested Taken by the police to a police station and made to stay there to answer questions about illegal activity.

assault The criminal act of using physical force against someone or of attacking someone.

Bank Holidays Public holidays – often on Mondays – when all banks and most businesses must close.

betting shop A place where a person can go and pay money to try to win money by gambling on the result of a horse race or football match etc.

Bill A parliamentary Bill is a statute in draft. That is to say, it has not yet become law.

binge drinking Drinking alcohol in great quantities in one session. Binge drinking, especially by young people, is currently the cause of much debate and concern.

Birth Certificate An official document that states the name of the person, the place and date of his or her birth and the names and occupations of their parents.

bishop A bishop is a senior church figure – below an Archbishop.

bonfire Bonfire night is another name for Guy Fawkes Night, celebrated on 5 November. The actual bonfire is an outdoor fire watched by people celebrating Guy Fawkes Night. An effigy of Guy Fawkes is often burned on the bonfire.

Boxing Day Boxing Day is a national holiday. Traditionally it was when people gave gifts (boxes) to servants and trades people, which is where it gets its name. It is celebrated on 26 December – the day after Christmas.

British Empire The British Empire was made up of countries colonised by Britain. This included countries in Africa, Asia, Australasia and North America.

Budget A document in which the Chancellor of the Exchequer sets out his position on taxation, benefits and the country's economy.

building society A kind of bank where money can be saved or from which money can be borrowed in order to buy a house (this borrowed money would be called a mortgage).

By-election This is an election held when an MP dies or resigns. It only involves the constituency of the MP concerned.

Cabinet The Cabinet comprises about 20 Government Ministers who decide government policy in their weekly meetings. It is usually chaired by the Prime Minister.

cannabis An illegal drug that is usually smoked.

canvas Another term for trying to get someone's support and particularly applies during election campaigns.

census A compulsory government count of the number of people in the country, to be completed by all households. It is carried out every ten years and gives the government information such as the number of residents, their religion, age and so on.

Chancellor of the Exchequer A senior minister responsible for the government's economic policy. He or she produces a 'Budget' in which current results, new measures and policies are announced. For instance, the Chancellor of the Exchequer would use the Budget speech to announce changes in taxation.

civil partnership This is when two people of the same sex legalise their relationship. In legal terms, a civil partnership is the same as marriage.

Civil Service Members of the Civil Service carry out the administrative duties of the government. They are independent of any political party.

coalition A partnership between different political parties.

cockney This refers to the regional accent of someone who lives in London.

Common Market What the European Union used to be called by many people.

Commonwealth An international organisation that came about as the British Empire crumbled. It includes 53 states.

constituency The area that an MP represents in parliament. All the people on the electoral register in a constituency are entitled to vote for the MP to represent them.

constitution A set of rules that controls how a country is governed. These rules can be written down or unwritten.

constructive criticism Criticism that helps a situation and is not simply damaging. One of the Opposition's main purposes is to offer constructive criticism of the government.

controlled drugs Illegal drugs including cannabis, heroin and cocaine.

convention A rule that is followed even though it is usually not written down.

coronation The act of crowning a new monarch. Queen Elizabeth the Second became Queen – the Monarch – when her father died in 1952 and the event was celebrated with her coronation in 1953.

Council of Europe The aim of the Council of Europe is to protect human rights and deal with European issues. It is made up of 46 member states.

Council of Ministers This is another European Union body. It makes decisions regarding how the EU is run and proposes new laws. It is made up of Ministers from EU states.

currency A particular system of money that a country – or group of countries – use. For example, in the European Union the euro is the form of currency that is most widely used.

democratic country A country which is governed by people who are elected by the population to represent them in parliament

denomination This refers to a branch of a religion. For example, Baptists are a Christian denomination.

devolved administration This is where power is passed from central government to regional institutions. Examples are the Scottish Parliament or the Welsh Assembly.

divorce This is the ending, in legal terms, of a marriage.

draft Bill The preliminary outline of a piece of legislation.

ecstasy A type of drug that is illegal and dangerous.

electoral register The list of all the people in an area who are entitled to vote in elections.

electorate All the people who are allowed to vote in an election.

ethnic minority A group of people who are of a different race from the race of the majority of the population of a country.

European Commission The organisation responsible for running the EU. It is based in Brussels.

European Economic Community This is what the European Union used to be called.

European Union (the EU) An organisation of 27 member states set up with the aim of co-operating on a variety of issues – particularly economic matters.

Father Christmas A traditional, imaginary figure who children believe brings them presents at Christmas.

first-past-the-post The system used in elections in the UK that means that the party that gains the most seats in Parliament will form the government.

Football Association This is the body that runs football in England.

Foreign Secretary The Minister responsible for foreign policy in Britain and for managing Britain's relationship with other countries.

free press This means that the content of newspapers is not controlled by the government – the press is free to publish its opinions.

Gaelic The native language of Scotland.

general election An election to elect members of Parliament (MPs). General elections involve the whole country and take place at least every five years.

Geordie The regional accent of people who live in Tyneside in the North East of England.

Grand National A horse race with difficult fences for the horses to jump. It is held once a year in April.

Gunpowder Plot A plot to blow up the Houses of Parliament in 1605.

Guy Fawkes Night A celebration held on 5 November every year to celebrate the failure of the Gunpowder Plot.

Hansard The official record of everything that happens in Parliament.

hard drugs The most serious of the controlled drugs, such as heroin and cocaine.

hereditary peers Peers who inherited their positions from their ancestors. Hereditary peers used to make up the House of Lords.

higher education Education that students receive at college or university.

Home Secretary The minister in charge of law and order and immigration.

House of Commons The lower Parliamentary chamber where MPs carry out their duties.

House of Lords The upper Parliamentary chamber where peers carry out their duties.

Houses of Parliament Both the House of Commons and the House of Lords. The Houses of Parliament are sometimes referred to as the Palace of Westminster, which is where it is situated.

iron curtain An imaginary line between Western and Eastern Europe until the downfall of the Soviet Union in the late 1980s.

judge The most important official in court, whose job it is to make sure that court proceedings are lawful and fair, and to decide what punishment to give a criminal if he or she is found guilty by the court.

jury Ordinary people (usually a group of 12) who listen to information in a court of law and then decide whether someone is guilty or innocent.

Kirk Another name for the Church of Scotland (Presbyterian Church).

Leader of the Opposition The leader of the second largest party in parliament.

legislation Laws and the process of making them.

life peers Peers appointed by the Prime Minister to sit in the House of Lords.

Lord Chancellor A member of the Cabinet responsible for the development and implementation of policy on the legal system. He is head of the judiciary and administers the courts and the legal system.

Lower House Another name for the House of Commons.

magistrate A person who acts as a judge in a court case where the crime is less serious than those tried by a judge.

media 'The media' means the newspapers and broadcasting companies.

mediation Advice and support given by a person or organisation to end an argument between two other people, or groups of people, who cannot agree.

Member of Parliament (MP) The representative of a constituency who has been elected to sit in the House of Commons.

Metropolitan Police The police force that serves London – the largest force in the country.

minister A senior government official with particular responsibilities.

Monarch The Queen or King

mortgage A loan, usually from a building society or bank, that is used to help to buy a house or flat.

Mothering Sunday A day of celebration in honour of mothers, held in March every year. Children buy gifts and cards for their mothers on this day.

mugging A criminal act that takes place in the street, in which someone steals by threat or by violence.

National Assembly for Wales The National Assembly for Wales is in Cardiff and is where Welsh representatives decide on policy.

National Curriculum The subjects that must be taught in state schools.

national day A day when a nation celebrates its country and its formation, e.g. St. David's Day in Wales.

naturalised citizen Someone who is born in one country but becomes a citizen of another country.

New Scotland Yard The headquarters of the Metropolitan Police in London.

non-departmental public bodies Agencies set up and funded by the government but with greater independence than government departments, e.g. Regional Development Agencies.

opposition The second largest party in Parliament, which is not in power as the government.

Palace of Westminster Where the Houses of Commons and Lords are situated.

Parliament Where MPs meet to carry out their duties.

Parliament of Scotland Where Scottish MPs meet to carry out their duties. Situated in Edinburgh.

parliamentary democracy This term describes a country where there is a system of elected representatives who make decisions about running the country.

party system A political system in which groups of people with common policies, values and aims form themselves in parties, e.g. Labour, Conservative etc.

patron saint A Christian saint who, according to religious belief, protects a particular place or group of people.

peers Members of the House of Lords

pogroms The intentional killing of people, usually because of their race or religious belief.

Pope The leader of the Roman Catholic Church.

Presbyterian Church Another name for the Church of Scotland.

prescription A note from a doctor saying which medicines a patient needs. The patient will take this to a pharmacy to buy the medicine.

pressure groups Groups with particular interests who seek to influence politicians to further their cause, e.g. the Animal Rights Movement or the Countryside Alliance

Prime Minister The leader of the party in government. He chairs the Cabinet.

proportional representation An electoral system in which seats in parliament are allocated according to the proportion of votes received by each political party.

Protestant A follower of the Christian religion who adheres to the principles established during the Reformation in 1534, when the Church of England broke away from the Roman Catholic Church.

quango A non-departmental government body.

Queen's Speech Delivered by the Queen (if we had a King, it would be called the King's Speech, of course) at the start of a new session of Parliament. It sets out the government's policies and what it plans to do in the coming session.

Question Time This is the time allocated in Parliament when MPs can ask questions of ministers.

redundant Someone becomes redundant when they are no longer needed to do a particular job. The person asked to leave may be entitled to money as compensation for the loss of their job (redundancy pay).

referendum A vote by the public or by a governing body to decide on a course of action or to make a political decision.

reformation This refers to the series of events that took pace in the 16th century, culminating in the Anglican Church breaking away from the Roman Catholic Church.

Remembrance Day This is held on 11 November each year to remember those who died in wars.

resign To officially announce a decision to leave a certain job.

retire To give up work, particularly later in life – usually between the ages of 60 and 65, or older.

Roman Catholic A member of the Christian religion who upholds the principles of the Church in Rome. The Church of England split from the Catholic Church as part of the Reformation.

Scouse This is the regional accent of people who live in Liverpool.

self-employed Someone who is self-employed works for themselves and not for an employer.

Shadow Cabinet A group of senior MPs belonging to the Opposition party who discuss policy and make decisions about important issues in the same way as the government's Cabinet – but without the power to enforce decisions in Parliament in this case.

solicitor A professional person whose job is to give legal advice and prepare documents for legal procedures.

Speaker The Speaker of the House acts as the chairperson during parliamentary debates. There is a speaker in both the House of Commons and in the House of Lords.

spin This is the slant put on news and announcements about political issues by spokespeople from the political parties.

St. Andrew's Day The national day of Scotland.

St. David's Day The national day of Wales.

St. George's Day The national day of England.

St. Patrick's Day The national day of Ireland – both Northern Ireland and the Republic of Ireland.

St. Valentine's Day This is the day when lovers and sweethearts send cards – sometimes anonymously – and flowers or chocolates to the person they love. It is celebrated on 14 February.

statute A permanent rule made by an organisation or institution for the government of its affairs.

stepfamily When two people, one or both of whom have children, remarry they form a new family known as a stepfamily.

Stormont The Northern Ireland Parliament is known as Stormont.

Supreme Governor The role fulfilled by the Monarch as Head of the Church of England.

trade union An association of workers that protects its members' rights at work.

treasury The government department that looks after the money that the government receives or pays out.

treaty An official written agreement between countries or governments.

unemployed Someone who is unemployed does not have a job and is not receiving any wages.

United Nations (UN) A multinational organisation set up after the Second World War to work for peace, human rights and security. It has 192 member states.

United Nations Security Council This is a committee of 15 members looking after world security. It has five permanent members of whom the United Kingdom is one.

Upper House This is what the House of Lords is sometimes called in Britain. The Upper House in a parliament reviews decisions made by the Lower House.

utilities Public utilities are services that the public can use, e.g. water, gas or electricity.

voluntary work Work that someone does because they want to and for which they do not receive payment.

welfare benefits Amounts of money paid by the government to people who have very little money and need help, perhaps because they are unable to work due to illness or disability.

Westminster This is the area where the Houses of Parliament are situated but is also used as a general term to describe the government.

whips Whips are MPs who have been appointed to ensure that other MPs in their party cast their votes in line with party policy.

Wimbledon This is an international tennis tournament held in June/July every year in south London.

Yellow Pages A book that lists names, addresses and telephone numbers of businesses, services and organisations in an area. There is also an online version.

The official material to be studied for the Life in the UK Test includes lots of dates in recent British history. Here, to help you remember them, is a list of the important ones.

Date	Event
1914	First World War begins.
1918	First World War ends.
1918	Women over 30 gain the right to vote for the first time.
1922	Parliament established in Northern Ireland when Ireland was divided.
1928	Women gain the right to vote at the same age as men.
1939	Second World War begins.
1940	Winston Church becomes Prime Minister – replacing Neville Chamberlain.
1945	Second World War ends.
1948	The National Health Service (NHS) begins.
1948	British Government invites people from the West Indies and Ireland to come to the UK to live and work.
1949	The Council of Europe is established.
1953	Coronation of Queen Elizabeth the Second.
1957	The Treaty of Rome is signed by six Western European countries, establishing the European Economic Community.
1957	The Prime Minister is allowed to appoint Life Peers for the first time.
1969	Young people are given the right to vote at the age of 18.

1969	The 'Troubles' break out in Northern Ireland.
1972	The Northern Ireland parliament is abolished because of the fighting taking place.
1973	Britain joins the European Union.
1979	The first referendum is held about forming a Scottish parliament.
1990	Margaret Thatcher resigns when she loses the support of her party.
1997	The second referendum is held about forming a Scottish parliament.
1998	The Good Friday Agreement – also known as the Belfast Agreement – is signed. This formed a basis for peace in Northern Ireland.
1999	Power is devolved from Westminster with the creation of the Scottish Parliament and the Assembly for Wales.
2001	A census is taken in the UK.
2002	Twelve European Union states adopt the euro as their common currency.
2004	Ten new member states join the European Union.
2007	Two more countries join the EU, bringing its total population to nearly half a billion.

teach® yourself

From Advanced Sudoku to Zulu, you'll find everything you need in the **teach yourself** range, in books, on CD and on DVD.

Visit **www.teachyourself.co.uk** for more details.

Advanced Sudoku and Kakuro
Afrikaans
Alexander Technique
Algebra
Ancient Greek
Applied Psychology
Arabic
Aromatherapy
Art History
Astrology
Astronomy
AutoCAD 2004
AutoCAD 2007
Ayurveda
Baby Massage and Yoga
Baby Signing
Baby Sleep
Bach Flower Remedies
Backgammon
Ballroom Dancing
Basic Accounting
Basic Computer Skills
Basic Mathematics
Beauty
Beekeeping
Beginner's Arabic Script
Beginner's Chinese Script
Beginner's Dutch

Beginner's French
Beginner's German
Beginner's Greek
Beginner's Greek Script
Beginner's Hindi
Beginner's Italian
Beginner's Japanese
Beginner's Japanese Script
Beginner's Latin
Beginner's Mandarin Chinese
Beginner's Portuguese
Beginner's Russian
Beginner's Russian Script
Beginner's Spanish
Beginner's Turkish
Beginner's Urdu Script
Bengali
Better Bridge
Better Chess
Better Driving
Better Handwriting
Biblical Hebrew
Biology
Birdwatching
Blogging
Body Language
Book Keeping
Brazilian Portuguese

Bridge
British Empire, The
British Monarchy from Henry
   VIII, The
Buddhism
Bulgarian
Business Chinese
Business French
Business Japanese
Business Plans
Business Spanish
Business Studies
Buying a Home in France
Buying a Home in Italy
Buying a Home in Portugal
Buying a Home in Spain
C++
Calculus
Calligraphy
Cantonese
Car Buying and Maintenance
Card Games
Catalan
Chess
Chi Kung
Chinese Medicine
Christianity
Classical Music
Coaching
Cold War, The
Collecting
Computing for the Over 50s
Consulting
Copywriting
Correct English
Counselling
Creative Writing
Cricket
Croatian
Crystal Healing
CVs
Czech
Danish
Decluttering
Desktop Publishing
Detox

Digital Home Movie Making
Digital Photography
Dog Training
Drawing
Dream Interpretation
Dutch
Dutch Conversation
Dutch Dictionary
Dutch Grammar
Eastern Philosophy
Electronics
English as a Foreign Language
English for International
   Business
English Grammar
English Grammar as a Foreign
   Language
English Vocabulary
Entrepreneurship
Estonian
Ethics
Excel 2003
Feng Shui
Film Making
Film Studies
Finance for Non-Financial
   Managers
Finnish
First World War, The
Fitness
Flash 8
Flash MX
Flexible Working
Flirting
Flower Arranging
Franchising
French
French Conversation
French Dictionary
French Grammar
French Phrasebook
French Starter Kit
French Verbs
French Vocabulary
Freud
Gaelic

Gardening
Genetics
Geology
German
German Conversation
German Grammar
German Phrasebook
German Verbs
German Vocabulary
Globalization
Go
Golf
Good Study Skills
Great Sex
Greek
Greek Conversation
Greek Phrasebook
Growing Your Business
Guitar
Gulf Arabic
Hand Reflexology
Hausa
Herbal Medicine
Hieroglyphics
Hindi
Hindi Conversation
Hinduism
History of Ireland, The
Home PC Maintenance and
  Networking
How to DJ
How to Run a Marathon
How to Win at Casino Games
How to Win at Horse Racing
How to Win at Online Gambling
How to Win at Poker
How to Write a Blockbuster
Human Anatomy & Physiology
Hungarian
Icelandic
Improve Your French
Improve Your German
Improve Your Italian
Improve Your Spanish
Improving Your Employability

Indian Head Massage
Indonesian
Instant French
Instant German
Instant Greek
Instant Italian
Instant Japanese
Instant Portuguese
Instant Russian
Instant Spanish
Internet, The
Irish
Irish Conversation
Irish Grammar
Islam
Italian
Italian Conversation
Italian Grammar
Italian Phrasebook
Italian Starter Kit
Italian Verbs
Italian Vocabulary
Japanese
Japanese Conversation
Java
JavaScript
Jazz
Jewellery Making
Judaism
Jung
Kama Sutra, The
Keeping Aquarium Fish
Keeping Pigs
Keeping Poultry
Keeping a Rabbit
Knitting
Korean
Latin
Latin American Spanish
Latin Dictionary
Latin Grammar
Latvian
Letter Writing Skills
Life at 50: For Men
Life at 50: For Women

Life Coaching
Linguistics
LINUX
Lithuanian
Magic
Mahjong
Malay
Managing Stress
Managing Your Own Career
Mandarin Chinese
Mandarin Chinese Conversation
Marketing
Marx
Massage
Mathematics
Meditation
Middle East Since 1945, The
Modern China
Modern Hebrew
Modern Persian
Mosaics
Music Theory
Mussolini's Italy
Nazi Germany
Negotiating
Nepali
New Testament Greek
NLP
Norwegian
Norwegian Conversation
Old English
One-Day French
One-Day French – the DVD
One-Day German
One-Day Greek
One-Day Italian
One-Day Portuguese
One-Day Spanish
One-Day Spanish – the DVD
Origami
Owning a Cat
Owning a Horse
Panjabi
PC Networking for Small
  Businesses

Personal Safety and Self
  Defence
Philosophy
Philosophy of Mind
Philosophy of Religion
Photography
Photoshop
PHP with MySQL
Physics
Piano
Pilates
Planning Your Wedding
Polish
Polish Conversation
Politics
Portuguese
Portuguese Conversation
Portuguese Grammar
Portuguese Phrasebook
Postmodernism
Pottery
PowerPoint 2003
PR
Project Management
Psychology
Quick Fix French Grammar
Quick Fix German Grammar
Quick Fix Italian Grammar
Quick Fix Spanish Grammar
Quick Fix: Access 2002
Quick Fix: Excel 2000
Quick Fix: Excel 2002
Quick Fix: HTML
Quick Fix: Windows XP
Quick Fix: Word
Quilting
Recruitment
Reflexology
Reiki
Relaxation
Retaining Staff
Romanian
Running Your Own Business
Russian
Russian Conversation

Russian Grammar
Sage Line 50
Sanskrit
Screenwriting
Second World War, The
Serbian
Setting Up a Small Business
Shorthand Pitman 2000
Sikhism
Singing
Slovene
Small Business Accounting
Small Business Health Check
Songwriting
Spanish
Spanish Conversation
Spanish Dictionary
Spanish Grammar
Spanish Phrasebook
Spanish Starter Kit
Spanish Verbs
Spanish Vocabulary
Speaking On Special Occasions
Speed Reading
Stalin's Russia
Stand Up Comedy
Statistics
Stop Smoking
Sudoku
Swahili
Swahili Dictionary
Swedish
Swedish Conversation
Tagalog
Tai Chi
Tantric Sex
Tap Dancing
Teaching English as a Foreign
    Language
Teams & Team Working
Thai
Theatre
Time Management
Tracing Your Family History
Training

Travel Writing
Trigonometry
Turkish
Turkish Conversation
Twentieth Century USA
Typing
Ukrainian
Understanding Tax for Small
    Businesses
Understanding Terrorism
Urdu
Vietnamese
Visual Basic
Volcanoes
Watercolour Painting
Weight Control through Diet &
    Exercise
Welsh
Welsh Dictionary
Welsh Grammar
Wills & Probate
Windows XP
Wine Tasting
Winning at Job Interviews
Word 2003
World Cultures: China
World Cultures: England
World Cultures: Germany
World Cultures: Italy
World Cultures: Japan
World Cultures: Portugal
World Cultures: Russia
World Cultures: Spain
World Cultures: Wales
World Faiths
Writing Crime Fiction
Writing for Children
Writing for Magazines
Writing a Novel
Writing Poetry
Xhosa
Yiddish
Yoga
Zen
Zulu

teach yourself

english as a foreign language
sandra stevens

- Do you know some English already?
- Do you want to learn more at home?
- Do you want to communicate with confidence?

English uses a special method to help you understand, speak and write English without a teacher. The course contains realistic dialogues, clear and simple explanations, lots of practice in communication, grammar and pronunciation, answers to common questions, and revision tests. Learn English where and when you want to!

Sandra Stevens has worked in EFL for over 30 years, as a teacher, teacher-trainer, writer and consultant.

teach
yourself

correct english
b. a. phythian & albert rowe

- Do you need help with writing English?
- Do you want a guide to the rules of grammar, punctuation and spelling?
- Do you worry that you sometimes make mistakes?

Correct English is a practical guide and reference book which will help you to improve your command of both spoken and written English, whether you are preparing for an English examination or simply want to improve your language skills. Learn how to avoid the commonest mistakes and pitfalls and increase your confidence to write letters, summaries, reports and essays.

B. A. Phythian's classic has been extensively simplified and updated by **Albert Rowe**, an experienced English teacher of many years.

teach
yourself

politics
peter joyce

- Do you want to understand key political terms and concepts?
- Would you like to consider important political questions?
- Are you looking for an introduction to this fascinating subject?

Politics gives you the background knowledge that enables you
to consider important political questions. Focusing on the
political systems operating in democratic states, it will give you
an understanding of these systems and the key terms, themes
and influences. Fully updated to include discussion of the
latest developments in politics and international relations, this
book is essential reading for all those who want to understand
politics today.

Peter Joyce is the Principal Lecturer in the department of
Sociology at Manchester Metropolitan University.